Grade Seven

Music Theory

(ABRSM Syllabus)

GRADE SEVEN MUSIC THEORY COURSE AND EXERCISES

By Victoria Williams

www.mymusictheory.com

1st Edition

ISBN-13: 978-1530907359

ISBN-10: 1530907357

CONTENTS

INTRODUCTION

This book was written for students who are preparing to take the ABRSM Grade Seven Music Theory exam. Parents of younger students will also find it helpful, as well as busy music teachers who are trying to fit a lot of music theory teaching into a very short time during instrumental lessons.

Each topic is broken down into digestible steps, and for best results the lessons should be followed in the order they are presented, as the acquired knowledge is cumulative.

After each topic, you will find a page or so of practice exercises, to help you consolidate what you have learned. Answers are provided on the page following the exercises.

I also highly recommend purchasing ABRSM past papers before sitting an actual exam. These can be obtained from shop.abrsm.org, Amazon or your local sheet music reseller.

You are welcome to photocopy the pages of this book for your own use, or to use with your pupils if you are a music teacher.

ABOUT THE AUTHOR

Victoria Williams graduated with a BA Hons degree in Music from the University of Leeds, UK, in 1995, where she specialised in notation and musicology.

In 2007 she decided to open up music theory teaching to a worldwide platform, by creating www.mymusictheory.com, which initially offered free lessons for Grade 5 ABRSM Music Theory candidates. Over the years, the full spectrum of ABRSM theory grades has been added, making MyMusicTheory one of the only websites worldwide offering a comprehensive, free, music theory training programme aligned with the ABRSM syllabuses.

You can connect with Victoria Williams in the following ways:

www.mymusictheory.com

info@mymusictheory.com

www.facebook.com/mymusictheory

www.twitter.com/mymusictheory

https://www.youtube.com/user/musictheoryexpert

I. WHAT YOU NEED TO KNOW ABOUT CHORDS

ROMAN NUMERAL SYSTEM

This course uses the "extended Roman numeral" system for describing chords.

The Roman numerals from 1-7 are I, II, III, IV, V, VI, VII.

I = tonic chord

II = supertonic chord

III = mediant chord

IV = subdominant chord

V = dominant chord

VI = submediant chord

VII = leading note chord

Capital letters are used for chords which contain a **major third** above the root, i.e. major and augmented chords. Lower case letters are used for chords which contain a **minor third** above the root, i.e. minor and diminished chords.

Augmented chords are differentiated from major chords by the use of a + symbol, and diminished chords are differentiated from minor chords by the use of a ° symbol.

Inversions are shown by the lower case letters a, b, c and d.

a = root position   c = second inversion

b = first inversion   d = third inversion (for four-note chords)

Numbers written after a Roman numeral are extra notes added on to the chord, for example the 7th. Chords (and added numbers) can be altered chromatically with accidentals, when necessary.

SOME EXAMPLES

If the key is A minor and the chord referred to is V7c, it is a dominant, E major chord with an added 7th (D) in second inversion (the bass note is B).

If the key is C major and the chord referred to is B°♭7b, it is a diminished 7th chord built on the leading note (B-D-F-Ab) in first inversion (bass note D). Read the chord as "B°" = B diminished (B-D-F), then "♭7" = with an added flattened 7th (Ab), then "b" = in first inversion (bass note D).

CHORDS IN MAJOR KEYS

The chords built on each degree of a major scale are as follows.

PRIMARY: I major   IV major   V major

SECONDARY: ii minor   iii minor   vi minor   vii° dim

CHORDS IN MINOR KEYS

Due to the melodic minor scale variants, there are more possible chords in minor keys.

PRIMARY: i minor   iv minor   V major

SECONDARY: ii° dim   III major   III+ aug   v minor   VI major   VII major   vii° dim

II. HOW TO HEAR MUSIC IN YOUR HEAD

You will vastly increase your chances of doing well in the grade 7 music theory exam, if you are able to hear printed music in your head.

Being able to hear music in your head is something that practically everybody can do. If you've ever had an "earworm" - a song which gets stuck in your head - for example, then you have the ability.

Or if I said to you, how does your National Anthem go? Can you hear yourself singing it in your head?

Most people can, even if you're not a very good singer! Try this one - can you hear an interval of a perfect 5th in your head?

Here's a harder one - can you hear a major chord being played on a piano?

The chances are that you managed all of those tasks. If you found the last two harder, don't worry - you have a bit more work to do, but the important thing is you DO have the ability - you just need to practise systematically.

RELATIVE PITCH

In all the tasks I just gave you, I wasn't asking you to find a **specific** pitch. I didn't ask you to, for example, start your National Anthem on a C, or hear a perfect 5th made from D and A. Being able to do that requires **perfect** pitch, which is something you tend to be either born with or without. Having perfect pitch is not at all necessary for our purposes. Actually, some people with perfect pitch find it a nuisance! In any case, what you need to develop is your **relative** pitch, and also your ability to hear simultaneous notes in your head.

HOW TO GET STARTED

Being able to read printed music in your head begins with being able to pitch intervals well. A single line of melody is just a series of intervals, at the most basic level. If you've taken any practical music exams, you might have had to recognise intervals by listening to them - if so, you have a head start!

The basic process for training your brain to hear intervals on paper, is to begin with what you know and progress in small steps. For each interval, you should start by picking a sound you want to hear it as - an instrument sound, or your own voice - use whatever comes naturally for now.

Next, look at the written interval and play the first note (e.g. on the piano), so you are starting in the right place, then try to sing the second note in your head. Then, immediately play the entire interval on your piano, or whatever instrument you have to hand, to check whether you were right.

Whether you were right or wrong, sing the correct note aloud, then immediately try to hear yourself echoing what you just sang, inside your head.

WHAT TO PRACTISE

It's a good idea to start with the consonant intervals, then move on to dissonant intervals with a diatonic key, then "chromatic" intervals.

Begin with listening to the intervals melodically – one note **after** the other. When you feel ready, move on to listening to the notes playing **simultaneously** (harmonic intervals).

When you've mastered hearing two notes at the same time, move on to triads.

Consonant Intervals

- Major and minor 3rd
- Perfect 4th
- Perfect 5th

- Major and minor 6th
- Perfect octave

Dissonant Intervals

- Major and minor 2nd
- Major and minor 7th
- Augmented 4th/diminished 5th

Common "Chromatic" Intervals (in the sense that they don't exist within the major or natural minor scale)

- Augmented 2nd/Diminished 7th (sounds like a minor 3rd/major 6th)
- Augmented 5th/Diminished 4th (sounds like a minor 6th/major 3rd)

USING A PHYSICAL REACTION

Many people find that it's easier to hear in their head if they imagine a physical action to go with each note.

For example, if you play the piano, imagine your fingers pressing the piano keys, or if you play the flute, imagine both your fingers and how your mouth feels when you blow those notes.

When you sing out loud, your Adam's apple (laryngeal prominence) moves up and down noticeably when you change pitch. Place two fingers lightly on your throat, and sing two notes an octave apart. Now try a scale. When you sing in your head, if you concentrate on the movement of your Adam's apple, it's likely to help you pitch the note.

IDEAS FOR PRACTICE

It can be really useful to make a list of songs you know that start with each of the most common intervals, up to an octave. It's best to pick songs you yourself know really well, but here are some examples.

Major 2nd: Happy Birthday to You

Perfect 4th: We Wish You a Merry Xmas

Augmented 4th/diminished 5th: "Maria" from West Side Story

Perfect octave: Somewhere Over the Rainbow

You can take a look at http://www.earmaster.com/products/free-tools/interval-song-chart-generator.html for some more ideas.

Another important point is that rhythm is really secondary when you are working on your inner ear. When you're practising, just work as slowly as necessary.

And in the same way, when you're trying to actually hear a score in head, it's usually best to work out the pitches first. You can easily tap out a rhythm silently with your foot or fingertips, so don't worry about fitting the rhythm in afterwards.

Finally, some proven exercises for increasing your ability to hear in your head is to do things the old-fashioned way. Before you dismiss these ideas as "old hat", I challenge you to have a go, and see for yourself!

- Copying out scores.

You can find free "classical" music scores at http://www.imslp.org (completely legal). Find the score of a piece you know (start with something simple – piano music or a duet), and copy out ten or twenty bars. As you do so, try to hear what you are writing. If you can use a music software program to do this, and use the playback feature for instant feedback, it's even more useful!

- Aural dictation

Try to write down the tunes of some songs or pieces you know well. Check on the piano when you've finished. Start with simple songs, children's nursery rhymes, Christmas Carols or TV theme tunes are a good choice. When you've gained confidence, try something more challenging – something more chromatic (jazz?) or with lots of key changes.

SECTION 1 – FIGURED BASS

1. ABOUT THE GRADE 7 FIGURED BASS QUESTION

Question 1 in the ABRSM grade 7 music theory exam asks you to add figures to a given bass line.

- This lesson gives you a brief outline of the exam question.

- The following lessons explain in detail what you need to know to tackle this question.

- The last lesson in this section shows you how to apply that knowledge to answer this question successfully.

If you follow the advice in these lessons, you should be able to figure a bass line so that it closely matches what is given in the ABRSM's model answers. In brief, this is how the question works – each point below will be explained in full in the following lessons.

- You will be given a complete bass line and melody line.

- The notes are written out in "piano" style, i.e. the stems of the notes obey the normal rules for piano music, rather than an SATB stave.

Piano style   SATB style

- A few chords at the beginning will already be figured. Asterisks are then placed under each bass note to show you where you need to add a figured bass.

- You need to understand how figures work, and the rules of harmony.

- You need to discover the tonality of the piece: what key is starts in, and what other keys it modulates through.

- Then you need work out which chords (including the inversion) fit the **chord notes.**

- When more than one chord fits, you should pick the **most likely** chord.

- The harmonic "vocabulary" which you are expected to use (i.e. which chords) is all the primary triads (I, V, IV), and the secondary triads II, III, VI and VII.

- In addition, you will probably have to use V7 and possibly II7. Other 7th chords might crop up, but V and II are the most common.

- You might need to include suspensions.

- If there is a harmonic sequence, you are advised to follow it.

2. REVISION OF CHORDS

Everything you learnt about chords at grade 6 also applies at grade 7, plus the "harmonic vocabulary" you are expected to know is extended to include chords with an added 7th. We'll study 7th chords in the next lesson; for now, here's a quick refresher on basic chords.

5-3: ROOT POSITION

- Root position chords have the figure 5-3, but these numbers are usually left out unless the chord is part of a progression which includes a **second** inversion (6-4) chord.

- 5-3 chords have the root of the triad in the bass (e.g. **C**-E-G)

- If possible, double the root. It's ok to double the 5th. It's only ok to double the 3rd in a **minor** chord, or in the specific progression V-VI (both major chords).

- Diminished chords are not normally used in root position.

- Root position chords are always preferred at important cadences.

1. Example 5-3 chord.

2. The 5-3 chord (boxed) is usually left un-figured in practice.

3. The 5-3 chord is always figured when it appears after a 6-4 chord.

6-3: FIRST INVERSION

- First inversion chords have the figure 6-3, which is normally abbreviated to 6.

- 6-3 chords have the third of the triad in the bass (e.g. **E**-G-C).

- In a major or minor chord, any note can be doubled, except the leading note.

- Diminished chords should always be in first inversion, with the bass doubled.

1. Example 6-3 chord.

2. The 6-3 chord (boxed) is usually figured with just a 6.

6-4: Second Inversion

- Second inversion chords are always notated in full with 6-4.

- 6-4 chords have the fifth of the triad in the bass (e.g. **G**-C-E)

- The bass note (which is the fifth of the triad) must be doubled. No other note can be doubled.

- 6-4 chords can only be used in special circumstances. Most often this means a **cadential 6-4**, or a **passing 6-4.** For more on this, see lesson 5 on common progressions.

1. Example 6-4 chord.

2. 6-4 chord used in a cadential 6-4.

Accidentals

Accidentals are added to figures to show that one of the upper parts (soprano, alto or tenor) will need an accidental.

Accidentals next to numbers in the figured bass refer to that interval above the bass.

Here, the interval a 6th above the bass (=F) needs to be sharpened.

Accidentals which appear on their own (without a number) always apply to the **third** above the bass note.

The third above the bass is G – so it becomes G#.

ILLEGAL CONSECUTIVES

A perfect 5th or a perfect octave between any two parts (soprano, alto, tenor or bass) must **never** be followed by another interval of the same type.

In the first pair of chords, there is a consecutive perfect fifth between the alto and tenor parts (boxed). The second pair of chords shows how this can be corrected – by changing the doubling of the C major chord in this case.

HORIZONTAL LINE

A horizontal line shows that the same chord still applies.

The A (bass) and C (soprano) are part of the (unfigured) 5-3 chord (A minor). The horizontal line shows that the D doesn't require a change of chord (it's a non-chord note).

2. REVISION OF CHORDS – EXERCISES

EXERCISE 1

Write the figures underneath the bass line for this full realisation. Leave 5-3 chords blank unless they are part of a 6-4 progression or chromatically altered. Remember to include any necessary accidentals.

EXERCISE 2

Find and circle five mistakes in this realisation. The mistakes are as follows:

    a.   An illegal consecutive 5th
    b.   An illegal consecutive octave
    c.   A incorrectly realised figure
    d.   One chord with incorrect doubling
    e.   One chord with an illegal missing triad note

2. REVISION OF CHORDS – ANSWERS

(accented passing note)

Notes:

An accidental which is not next to a number always refers to the third above the bass. The final figure shows that there is a C#; the F# occurs in the key signature, so the # is not included in the figure.

EXERCISE 2

Notes:

The doubled third in the Bb major chord in bar 1 is allowed, because it is part of the V-VI progression. When V moves to VI, doubling the 3rd in VI avoids consecutives and awkward augmented movement.

In d, the chord is diminished, so the bass needs to be doubled.

In e, the 6-4 chord needs to include all three triad notes.

3. 7TH CHORDS

THE DOMINANT 7TH

The most important chord in any key is the **tonic**. The second most important chord is the **dominant**. In the key of C major, for example, the chord of G major is the dominant chord. These two chords work together to **fix the key** of a piece of music. In tonal music, the tonic-dominant relationship is absolutely the most important relationship that there is, and therefore we find many V-I or I-V progressions throughout any piece of music (in the period we are studying, which is late Baroque to Classical).

In a V-I progression, it is the magnetism of the **semitone pull** from the leading note to the tonic which creates the power of the progression. We feel that the leading note **has to** be followed by the tonic, to release the tension which has built up. Here, the leading note B has a strong pull towards the tonic C:

The magnetism of the semitone can be increased, by adding a **7th** to the dominant chord. The 7th is calculated from the root of the triad. In this case, it's a G major chord, so the 7th is F.
The result is **two semitones** with magnetic pulls. The 7th (F here) falls to the mediant of the tonic chord.

- Dominant 7th chords occur frequently **within** a piece of music, but are less common at important cadences, where the basic V-I progression is often preferred.

- Dominant 7th chords occur very frequently when music is **modulating**. When music changes key, it is necessary to use chords which fix the new key without any ambiguity. The only chords able to do this are V and I (in the new key). V7-I allows a richer harmony.

- V7 chords are nearly always followed by a chord I, but V7-VI is also used.

This example starts in C major (chord I). The next chord (D7) is V7 in G major – the music is **modulating** to the dominant key. The final G major chord is chord I (in G major).

Secondary 7ths

You can add a 7th on to any chord. The **dominant 7th** has such an important place in the way that harmony functions, that it is the only "primary" 7th chord. If you add a 7th on to any other chord, it is known as a "**secondary 7th**".

The most common secondary 7th found in this grade 7 question is **ii7**. It is no coincidence that chord ii is actually the "dominant of the dominant", being a fifth higher!

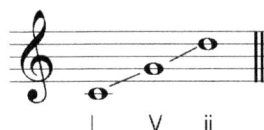

Chord ii7 leads very nicely on to chord V, so you will often find a ii7-V-I progression. The supertonic 7th chord is found in both the minor and major versions. In the example below, the bass note can be F or F#.

Notating 7ths in Figured Bass

Since there are **four** notes in added 7th chords, it should come as no surprise that there are four ways you can write them: root position, plus 1st, 2nd and **3rd** inversions. (3rd inversion is notated as "d" in Roman numerals). The abbreviated figures are normally used:

Root position (a): 7 (short for 7-5-3)

1st inversion (b): 6-5 (short for 6-5-3)

2nd inversion (c): 4-3 (short for 6-4-3)

3rd inversion (d): 4-2 (short for 6-4-2)

You can learn these figures in less than a minute. Notice the pattern:

7 – 65 – 43 – 2

All you need to remember is that you should add a "4" to the last figure to make "4-2". The other numbers are just the descending numbers from 7.

You will see some of the "missed out numbers" reappear if they need accidentals added to them, or if they cannot be omitted from the chord. (There's an example later in this lesson).

Here are the four inversions of the dominant 7th chord in C major:

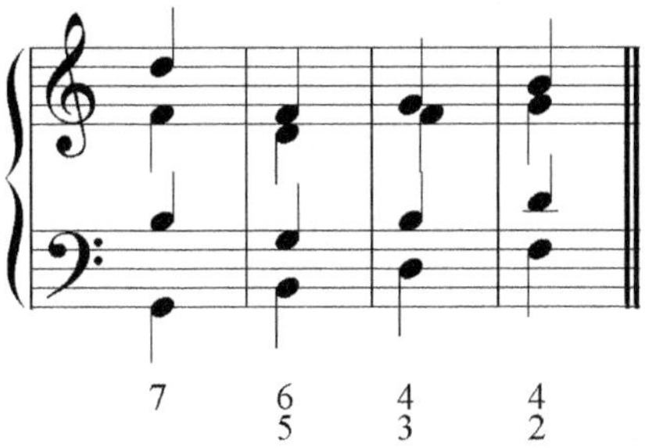

As with any figures, accidentals can be added. An accidental which appears without a number applies to the **third** above the bass. Because 7th chords are often added when music is changing key, you can expect lots of accidentals thrown in!

Here's an example for you to play. Starting in C major, the music quickly modulates through D minor then E minor:

Here's the same music with the bass figured:

The second chord has a "floating" sharp which means the third above the bass (C) must be sharpened.

The fourth chord has a 5#, meaning the fifth above the bass (F) must be sharpened, and a "floating" sharp, which means the third, D, is also sharpened. This is an example of the "missed out" 5 reappearing in the figure, because it's been altered chromatically. Both of these 7th chords are root position.

Each note of a chord should move gracefully to the next note in the same part. You will have studied some rules of voice-leading during the grade 6 course.

For example, the soprano often moves by **step**, the alto and tenor parts should move as **little as possible or not at all**, and the bass often has a fall of a **4th** or leap of a **5th**.

In the first example below, the voice-leading is good. The soprano part moves by a second (a "step"), as does the tenor part. The alto part repeats the same note, and the bass falls by a 4th.

In the second example, the alto and tenor parts have poor voice-leading.

Good!   Bad!

The rules of voice-leading tell us that if two notes are a **semitone** apart, they should normally be kept in the **same** part. The two semitones created by a V7 chord need to be treated carefully!

The 7th in an added 7th chord should always fall by step.

This is important to know, even though you are not asked to write out the middle harmony parts in the grade 7 exam, because it means that V and V7 chords are **not necessarily interchangeable**.

In the grade 7 theory exam figured bass question, you are given a bass line and melody line and are asked to suggest figures for the bass. Sometimes you might consider V or V7, thinking they are more or less the same. The voice-leading, however, can cause problems. You need to check the melody line to make sure a V7 chord would work. Here's an example.

Key: A major

The G# and E in chord 1 might fit with Vb (E major) or V7b (E7), and chord 2 is Ia (A major). To check if the V7 chord would work, **sketch in the missing notes** and work out where they should move to, according the rules of voice-leading:

Key: A major

The added 7th in chord 1 would be D. D would have to fall to C#, because it's a semitone pull. This would create two C#s in the A major chord, but doubling the third in a major chord is not allowed. Therefore, chord V7 won't work here. Chord V is fine though.

The Clue's in the Question

An easy way to spot where a 7th chord is intended is to identify a bass note and melody note which are a **2nd** (compound) apart. Here's an example – look at the chord marked 1.

The bass note is G and the melody note is A – they are a compound 2nd apart. You need to figure out which chord contains both of these notes – only a 7th chord can contain two notes which are a (compound) 2nd apart. In this case it is Am7 – or ii7d. The chord notes are A-C-E-G. (Remember that in a 7th chord, there are four notes which are a third apart from each other, and the lowest of these is the chord root.)

This is how you could figure the above progression (alto and tenor parts also added for reference):

3. 7TH CHORDS – EXERCISES

EXERCISE 1

All of these chords are added 7th chords. Figure them correctly, including any necessary accidentals in the figure.

EXERCISE 2

The following are all V7 - I (or i) progressions. Name each chord e.g. G7 - C major. An example is given.

EXERCISE 3

a. For each pair of chords, state whether the **first** chord could be figured with:

- A. **V (only)**,
- B. **V7 (only)** or
- C. **Either V or V7**

(Remember that you shouldn't use a V7 chord if the best voice-leading creates illegal consecutives/doubling).

3. 7TH CHORDS – ANSWERS

EXERCISE 1

EXERCISE 2

a.   B7 – E minor

b.   C7 – F minor

c.   F#7 – B minor

d.   A7 – D minor

e.   F7 – Bb major

f.   C#7 – F# minor

EXERCISE 3

a.   Either V or V7

b.   V7 only

c.   V only

d.   V7 only

4. SUSPENSIONS

WHAT IS A SUSPENSION?

A suspension happens when a note from one chord is **held** over (or repeated) into the following chord, making a **dissonance** with the bass. The dissonance then **resolves** to a consonance.

V7a   Ia

- Here, the F from the previous V7a chord is repeated in the Ia chord. Remember that F doesn't normally belong in a C major chord!

- The F forms a **dissonance** with the bass. Intervals which are dissonant with the bass are the 2nd, 4th, and 7th (and their compounds). Dissonances feel kind of "crunchy".

- The dissonant note (F) **resolves** onto E (crunchy becomes smooth). E is part of the normal C major chord, so it is **consonant**.

HOW TO FIGURE A SUSPENSION

In figured bass, **both** the suspension and resolution need to be figured.

- In the above example, the "alien" note in the C major chord is a 4th above the bass, so we figure it with a 4.

- The 4th above the bass (F) moves ("resolves") to the third above the bass (E), so we figure that with a 3.

- The two notes of the suspension are connected with a short dash

4 — 3

In the Grade 7 music theory exam figured bass question, it's usually relatively easy to spot where a suspension is needed. You will find that the bass note does **not** change (but might leap by an octave), but there are **two** asterisks (used to show where the ABRSM wants you to put a figure) below the bass note. Something like this:

The bass note E has two asterisks.

Note that the bass line could also look like this if a 6-4 chord is required, rather than a suspension. Look at the melody notes carefully – in the above case it can't be a 6-4 chord on the E bass, because the other chord notes would be C and A.

Next, check that the suspended note was part of the **previous** chord. The previous chord here is A minor (because it's unfigured, so it's a 5-3 chord). Of the notes A, C and E, only A makes a dissonance with a bass E (it's a 4th). So the suspension must be 4-3.

Watch out! In a minor key, most V chords should be major-ised. This suspension will resolve on to a chord of E **major**, so we'll need to add an accidental to the figure too. Here's the bass figured:

And just for your information, this is how the full realisation might look:

Notice that in this case, the suspension occurs in an **inner part** (i.e. not in the melody line or bass). Although you don't actually need to write out the alto and tenor parts in the grade 7 exam, you do need to know what is likely to be happening within them!

What if we chose to figure this a different way? Perhaps we could put E major then A minor, or E major then C major? The first solution won't work, because the A minor chord would be in second inversion, but is not one of the cases where a second inversion chord will work. The second solution is also unsatisfactory, because E major followed by C major is not a common progression (see chapter 5).

Sometimes the bass line may appear NOT to be static – but remember that any added notes of melodic decoration **won't** affect the fundamental harmony. In this case, on the third beat of the bar, the bass moves from Eb down to Bb, then up to Eb again. But the Bb is incidental – (it's actually a "harmonic auxiliary note") – and the **fundamental bass** is just Eb.

In this suspension, the melody note Ab is first sounded in the first inversion Ab major chord (figured "6"). When the bass line moves up to Eb, the Ab in the melody becomes suspended. It's now figured with a 4, because Ab is a 4th above Eb. The Ab then resolves to G, which is the 3rd of the Eb major chord. The Bb in the bass line is another chord note from the Eb major chord – it is melodic decoration, but is not dissonant within the Eb major chord.

Suspensions can also occur in the bass line itself, although this isn't seen very often. Here's an example.

Bar 1 contains a D major chord, with D in the bass. In bar 2, the bass D is held over, but the harmony changes to an A major chord. The D resolves to C# in the second half of bar 2. It is figured with 5-2, "5" is the A above the bass and "2" is the E. The clues here are the **tied note** (tied and repeated notes are always a good clue that a suspension might be required), and the repeated E/A in the melody. Think of it as similar to the suspension with the decorated bass note shown in the last paragraph, but upside down.

Tip! Look for Patterns

Look carefully at the first couple of bars or so, which will already be figured for you. If you see suspensions figured within the opening, see if you can find a sequence somewhere in the rest of the piece, where the same shape of melody/bass line has been used (perhaps at a different pitch). If you find a short stretch of music which is similar, it's likely that a suspension will fit there too. The ABRSM **does** expect you to be looking for sequences and other similarities, and to treat them in similar ways. If there is an obvious sequence and you fail to use a similar harmony, you may lose points.

4. SUSPENSIONS – EXERCISES

1. Complete the table, which outlines the three parts of a suspension.

Name	Description
	The first sounding of a note which is going to be suspended.
Suspension itself	
	Note which follows the suspension itself.

2. Figure these bars containing basic suspensions, as marked by the asterisks.

3. Figure these bars which contain slightly more complex suspensions, as marked by the asterisks.

Don't forget that the suspended note must be prepared in the previous chord – but it could be in any of the parts (not just the visible ones!) If you are stuck, some tips are listed at the bottom of the page.

Tips:

The bass in a) includes melodic decoration.

In b) the suspension is in an inner part.

In c) it may help to imagine the bass line being above the soprano, to see how the suspension works.

4. SUSPENSIONS – ANSWERS

1. Complete the table, which outlines the three parts of a suspension.

Name	Description
Preparation	The first iteration of a note which is going to be suspended.
Suspension itself	The dissonant note, which is held from the previous chord.
Resolution	Note which follows the suspension itself.

2.

3.

Note that in the G major suspension, you need to figure it as 5-2, and not just 5. This is to ensure that the realised chord is D major with a suspended G, rather than G major.

5. COMMON PROGRESSIONS

Music composed in the era we are studying followed **standard patterns** of chords, known as "progressions". Lots of different melodies can be composed using the **same** chord pattern. (This is also true of modern pop music, but the chord patterns common in pop music are not always the same as those used in classical.)

Chord patterns are important to know, because if you need to choose between two possible chords, you should always choose the most **likely** chord (in the grade 7 exam).

CADENCES

Use a standard cadence whenever there is pause in the music, and at the end of any phrases.

A **pause** can be marked with a fermata (pause symbol), with a double bar line, with a long held chord, or even with a rest in all parts.

However, the **end of a phrase** might not be marked in any special way – you will need to work out the phrases based on the melody and any sequences. For example, the melody might be built from a 2-bar rhythm which is repeated at different pitches. The end of the phrase could happen in bar 4 and/or bar 8, (bars 4 and 8 are always a good place to look!)

The standard cadences are the **perfect** (V-I), **plagal** (IV-I), **imperfect** (anything – V) and **interrupted** (V-VI). In a minor key, chord V in a cadence is always **major** and will need the third raised by a semitone.

VI-II-V-I (THE PROGRESSION OF 5THS)

Each degree of the scale has its own dominant. Let's take the key of C major. Starting on the tonic (C), the dominant is G. Starting on G, the dominant is D. If we carry on in the same way, we get this: C-G-D-A-E-B-F#. Each note in this sequence is the **dominant** of the previous note. (You could keep on going, but Baroque/Classical composers generally didn't!)

Of these, the first 4 chords (I-V-ii-vi) are seen the most often in a progression – but in reverse order. So, the progression we frequently see is vi-ii-V-I. Any "dominant" could also have a 7th added on to it, so you could find ii7-V-I, or ii-V7-I, for example. (Avoid V7 at a cadence though). As dominants, they can be found in their major or minor forms.

Here is an example, the key is G major:

The notes in the bass line and melody allow us to use the circle of fifths progression vi-ii-V7-I, figured like this: (the inner parts are shown for reference only)

Chord Ic

The second inversion tonic chord needs to be used with care. It can only be used

- in a cadential 6-4

- in a passing 6-4

- in an auxiliary 6-4

Remember that if you use a 6-4 chord, you need to write out the figures of the 5-3 chord which follows in **in full** (i.e. don't leave the figure blank).

A **cadential 6-4** is the chord progression Ic-Va, and it is often (but not always) found, as the name suggests, at a cadence. Remember that a cadence is expected when the music pauses for a moment, at the end of a phrase or the end of a piece. In a cadential 6-4, the Ic chord always falls on a **strong** beat.

Chords Ic and Va have the same bass note. You can spot a place where a 6-4 progression will work by checking that the bass note is **the same** for two different successive chords. A long note might be used which covers both chords, there may be a repeated note, or there may be an octave difference. All of these bass lines would fit a Ic-Va progression:

(long note)   (repeated note) (octave difference)

A **passing 6-4** happens when the bass line moves by step. The 6-4 chords falls on a **weak** beat in this case. (The 6-4 chord acts like a passing note). An **auxiliary 6-4** also occurs on a weak beat, and is found when the bass note is an auxiliary note (a note which is one scale-step between two identical notes).

Passing 6-4   Auxiliary 6-4

In fact, it's quite rare that you will need to use either a passing or auxiliary 6-4 in this question. Unless you are sure about using them correctly, it's safer to avoid them. However, cadential 6-4's are very likely to come up, so make sure you know how they work!

The chord which happens immediately **before** a cadential 6-4 is very often iib. This is because the bass line moves by step, and it sounds nice!

It is worth remembering the cadential 6-4 as a longer sequence of iib-Ic-Va-Ia. Here is an example:

And here it is with the figures (and inner parts for reference):

VII° - I

Chord vii° is a "substitute dominant". Because it contains 3 of the same notes as chord V7, it can be used in many of the same places where V7 works. However, you shouldn't use it at a cadence – only chord V should be used in a proper perfect cadence. It is best to always follow vii° with I.

III AND VII

In a major key, chord iii is minor. It is not used very often, but can be found before chord vi as part of the circle of 5ths.

In a minor key, only a major chord III can be used (meaning that the leading note is not sharpened.) For example, in A minor, the leading note G is not sharpened to G# in chord III, the chord is C-E-G, a C major chord. Chord III is the relative major, and so is often found with the dominant chord in the relative major key, which is a major chord VII. So in A minor, you can find C major (III) with G major (VII). III also works with ii°b in a minor key, taking the key back to the relative minor.

V7 - Modulation

If the music changes key, chord V7 in the **new key** makes the modulation stronger.

Look carefully at the key signature at the start, and analyse what is happening in the melody. The addition of accidentals usually means a key change is taking place (although they can also be normal scale notes in a minor key, or simply added for decoration – check carefully).

Here is an example. The original key is D major, but at this point several G#s have been introduced. This tells us that the piece must be modulating to A major (to the dominant key). The last given chord (shaded) is Vb in the new key:

The next chord (with the first asterisk) would also fit with chord V in A major (root position), however as the music is changing key it would be much more satisfactory to use V7 instead. This would be followed by chord VIa (F# minor) (remember that V7 is usually followed only by I or VI).

This is how the figures look:

The root position 7th chord is notated with "7", but because the third of the chord has been sharpened (G#) we also have to add a sharp sign underneath. (Remember that accidentals which are written without a number always refer to the third above the bass). The next chord is left unfigured, as it is a 5-3 chord.

Summary of Progressions

Here is a brief summary of good progressions (many other progressions are allowed, but these are the most likely to fit!)

I > anything except III	III > VII, ii°b	VI > II
IIa > V	IV > I	VII > I
IIb > Ic	V > I or VI	

5. COMMON PROGRESSIONS – EXERCISES

For each of the following progressions numbered 1-3:

- name the **prevailing** key
- figure the bass line using the **most common progressions** (use figured bass)
- also write the chords using Roman numeral notation including inversion, below your figured bass

1.

2. There are two ways to figure the second chord here – can you find both? (They are in the same key).

3. These bars include a modulation, so give the prevailing key for **each** of the two bars, and circle the **pivot chord** (i.e. the chord which exists in both keys and is used to slide into the change of key).

5. COMMON PROGRESSIONS – ANSWERS

1. D major (suggested answer)

6 6 5
     4 3

iib Ic Va Ia

Note: Remember that you shouldn't use two identical chords next to each other, so Va-Va isn't possible.

Chord iii is not recommended as it is rarely used in this style.

Ic-Va is a typical cadential 6-4.

Chord IV (figure blank) also works for the first chord.

2. B minor (suggested answer)

6♯ 6   6♯ 6
           4

ia vii°b ib   ia Vc ib

Note: the key isn't D major, because of the doubled C# (you can't double the leading note).

Avoid chord ii°a, as diminished chords are normally used in first inversion.

The second working here includes a passing 6-4.

3. F major modulating to C major (or C minor).

6   6   7
          ♮

vib iia Vb Ia/IVa V7a Ia

Note: Use V7 (instead of V) as the last-but-one chord, to make a better modulation.

V7b would also be ok for the third chord.

38

6. MODULATION

At grade 7, it's very likely that the figured bass exercise you are given in the exam contains some **modulation**, or **passes through** different keys.

> ➢ A true **modulation** occurs when the music changes from one tonal centre to another, and stays there for some time. For example, a piece could start in A minor, modulate to E major and then continue in that key for a while. It's usually relatively easy to spot a modulation and work out which keys are involved.

> ➢ When a piece of music **passes through** various keys, it can sometimes take a little bit more detective work to figure out what's going on. When music passes through a key, that key might only last a very short while – even perhaps just one chord. And it's possible to move through several keys in quick succession.

RELATED KEYS

Music from this era (late Baroque/early Classical) usually moves to a **closely related key**, whether as a modulation, or just passing through.

The most closely related keys are the **dominant** and **subdominant**, the **relative** major/minor, and the **parallel** key. ("Parallel" keys are C **major** and C **minor**, for example. Any of the closely related keys can be used in its parallel form too.)

For example, if the piece begins in C major, then the most closely related keys are these:

- C minor (parallel key)
- A minor (relative minor)

- F major (subdominant)
- G major (dominant)

But, as soon as the key passes from C major to one of these related keys, it might either return to the **original** key, another **closely related key** or pass through the **next** level of related keys. Let's say C major passes through A minor. From this point, the next key to pass though could be related to C major again, or to A minor:

- A major (parallel key)
- C major (relative major)

- D minor (subdominant)
- E major (dominant)

And so on. So as you can see, you can move from C major to E major very quickly, although they are not closely related to each other.

It's also worth remembering that the dominant chord is occasionally used in its **minor** form (parallel), in a minor key. For example, in A minor, we would normally expect the dominant chord to be E major, and a modulation would be to the major key. But you could equally modulate from the key of A minor to E minor.

Spotting Key Changes

Usually you will easily be able to see where a key change is happening – there will be accidentals in the music which do not fit the current key. If the piece begins in C major and you see an F#, that is a good sign that the music is modulating to G major. Don't forget though, that accidentals can be used simply because the piece is in a minor key, or as chromatic melodic decoration.

There may be no visible accidentals, however, when the music moves between the relative major and minor, since they share a key signature.

Working out Key Changes

Once you have identified the place where a key change (or changes) is happening, you'll need to work out what that key is, so that the correct chord can be figured.

It's essential to remember that during this period, most key changes were created with the use of **chord V or V7** in the new key. (An exception is when the music moves into the parallel key: when C minor moves immediately to C major, for example.)

*Don't forget that chord **vii°** is considered to be a V7 substitute. The chord notes F#-A-C, for example, make up chord vii° in G major. V7 in G major is D-F#-A-C – it's the same as vii° with a missing root. In the following paragraphs, chord vii° also works wherever you see V7.*

Important: When used as a tool for modulation, the dominant chord will always be in its **major** form.

Let's go back to the list of closely related keys, and examine the chords which would be expected at those modulations.

C major > F major: via C (C-E-G) or C7 (C-E-G-Bb)

C major > G major: via D (D-F#-A) or D7 (D-F#-A-C)

C major > A minor: via E (E-G#-B) or E7 (E-G#-B-D)

In order to know which is the correct chord to figure at a modulation, follow these steps:

1. Work out the key up to this point, and list the **closely related** keys. This narrows down the possibilities!

2. Look at the bass and melody lines, and work out **which dominant/tonic chords would fit**, always remembering to think through the added 7th chords too.
    For example, a C/F# would fit D7, and B/G# would fit E or E7.
    In most cases, an **added 7th chord is preferable** when the key is changing, as it fixes the new key more strongly. This is particularly important when the key is changing rapidly.

3. Jot down the chord notes, paying attention to any **accidentals** which will be necessary to add to the figure.

4. Look at the next chord for confirmation. Usually, it will be chord I (or i) in the new key. But, there may be another key change to another closely related key instead.

This is the beginning of Bach's chorale no. 200, *"Christus ist erstanden, hat überwunden".* It starts in C major – this is apparent from the key signature and opening tonic chord.

Chord 2 is G major (V) in first inversion.

Chord 3 contains a suspension. The G is not a "member" of this chord – it's a hanger-on from chord 2. Chord 3 contains the notes A-C-F#, which is chord vii° in G major, so at this point the music is **passing though** G major.

Chord 4 is G major. But it includes an F natural passing note, making G-B-D-F, or V7 in the key of C major.

Chord 5 is C major (I), but again the passing note Bb then creates C-E-G-Bb, or C7 in F major.

Chord 6 is F major.

Chord 7 is C major, with a suspension. At this point, whether you name this as V in F major or I in C major is a matter of individual perception! After moving through so many keys so quickly, the original tonal centre (key) is lost, and the final chord has some ambiguity about it.

Now take a closer look at the **bass** and **soprano** lines – in fact, these parts don't include any of those added **accidentals**. If you were given this piece as an exercise, you could do it without any key changes at all. However, it's worth playing it through, to notice how Bach effectively changes key rapidly, and the effect of the added 7th chords. Play it through **without** the accidentals as well, and compare the results. It sounds fine, but it's much less interesting aurally.

Occasionally Bach changes to a less closely related key, e.g. in chorale 199 he moves from a chord of F7 immediately to G7. However, you're not likely to find such a progression in the grade 7 exam.

Now let's take a look at some typical exercises where a modulation is not optional. These two bars are taken from the middle of Bach's chorale no. 215, *"Verleih' uns Frieden gnädiglich"*. The key is G minor at the start of the extract.

Notice the C sharp, and also the F (natural) at the end of the second bar. These are clues that the key is changing.

Now find the most likely chord/key for each numbered chord.

Chord 1 is V(7) in G minor (6 or 6-5).

Chord 2 is i in G minor (5-3).

Chord 3 is V(7) in G minor (5-3# or 7#).

Chord 4 is i in G minor (cadence) (5-3). (G major would also work here).

Chord 5, with two G's, is i again (5-3). (Think through the alternatives and pick the most "usual" chord).

Chord 6 has C# and G, which are both in V7 in the key of D (dominant key). So this is V7 in D (6-5-♮).

Chord 7 has D and F natural, which confirms the modulation to D minor. This is i in D minor (5-3).

Chord 8 with Bb and G is open to interpretation. Look at the next chord for some clues.

Chord 9 with F and C will be an F major chord (5-3). We could then interpret the G/Bb in the previous chord as V7 (6♮-4-3-) or vii° (6♮) in F major – the relative major key. (In fact, Bach uses vii° and the chorale stays in F major for a few more beats.)

It can be helpful to try and assume the "**most likely scenario**", when you are faced with chords that could be interpreted in different ways. Chords 8 and 9 are a good example of this. The G/Bb in chord 8 could be interpreted as G minor, E° or C7. Chord 9 could be F major or minor. How do you choose the most likely combination?

Firstly, F **major** is more closely related to the previous key of D minor, than F **minor** is. F major is the relative key.

Having chosen F major for chord 9, which progression is more common: V7-I, vii°-I or ii-I? Either of the first two progressions is fine, but ii-I is relatively unusual, so choose V7 or vii°.

This is the opening of Bach's chorale no.206, *"So gibst du nun, mein Jesu, gute Nacht"*.

The key signature is two flats, and the F# in bar 1 should lead you to G minor as the opening key.

The first cadence, at chord 4, is clearly V7-i.

The F natural at the end of bar 1 is a diatonic note in G minor, because it's part of the melodic minor scale. By itself, it's not enough to signify a key change.

Take a look at chord 10 though – the pause symbol means this is another cadence (you can also look for longer note values, don't forget). But the two notes we have to work with are both Bb's. At a cadence, in the final chord we'd normally expect:

- A root position chord
- A doubled root

Which means that chord 10 should be a chord of Bb major.

Chord 9 has the notes A and C – which fit with chord V in Bb major (F major). However, the C in the bass would make Vc, but a second inversion chord would not be acceptable in this position. We should therefore make this a V7c chord. (7th chords can be used freely in second inversion).

6. MODULATION – EXERCISES

EXERCISE 1

Complete the following:

The extract begins in the key of _____ and modulates to the key of _____ by bar 4. The relationship of the new key to the old is: _____.

In bar 5 the presence of _____ is a clue that another key change is taking place. Bar 5 uses chord V7b followed by chord Ia in the key of _____. The relationship of this key to the original key is: _____.

Bar 6 uses chord _____ followed by chord _____ in the key of _____ The relationship of this key to the original key is: _____.

At the end of bar 6 we find chord _____ in the original key, leading back to the tonic chord of _____ on the first beat of bar 7. The piece ends with a _____ cadence.

EXERCISE 2

Add figured bass to the above score, using one chord on each asterisk. 5-3 chords should be left blank, unless they are part of a 6-4 5-3 progression or are chromatically altered.

6. MODULATION – ANSWERS

EXERCISE 1

The extract begins in the key of <u>E minor</u> and modulates to the key of <u>G major</u> by bar 4. The relationship of the new key to the old is: <u>relative major.</u>

In bar 5 the presence of <u>accidentals</u> is a clue that another key change is taking place. Bar 5 uses chord V7b followed by chord Ia in the key of <u>A major</u> The relationship of this key to the original key is: <u>parallel subdominant (or major subdominant).</u>

Bar 6 uses chord <u>V7b</u> followed by chord <u>Ia</u> in the key of <u>B major.</u> The relationship of this key to the original key is: <u>dominant.</u>

At the end of bar 6 we find chord <u>V7b</u> in the original key, leading back to the tonic chord of <u>E minor</u> on the first beat of bar 7. The piece ends with a <u>perfect</u> cadence.

EXERCISE 2 SUGGESTED ANSWER

Where an added 7th occurs as a passing note, (e.g. the C in bar 3), it can be difficult to know whether to include it in the figure or not. A good rule of thumb is to include the 7th in the figure if it is part of a modulation (it will strengthen the modulation), or if there is a pattern of 7ths in the melody, which it would be good to continue.

7. CHOOSING CHORDS

Working out which chord to use is the tricky part of figuring a bass. You need to keep in mind quite a lot of information:

- Work out what key the piece is in and make a note of any apparent modulations.

- Pick a chord which both the melody and bass is part of.

- Make sure that the inversion is allowed.

- Make sure that the progression is stylistically correct.

- Do the easy parts first and leave difficult chords until the end.

- Look for clues like a static bass line, or leading note/tonic in the melody.

- Look for patterns or sequences in the harmony, and keep them going when possible

CADENCES AND SUSPENSIONS FIRST

First scan through the piece looking for places where it's obvious that a **cadence** or **suspension** is needed. Cadences always happen at the end of a piece of course, but often they happen in the middle too.

Look for places where the bass line is **static** (or moves by an octave) but the melody moves by step – these are the places where **cadential 6-4s and suspensions** will be needed. (Don't forget that suspensions need to be prepared first). Do these first.

Here are the last two bars of a piece in A minor:

We will need a perfect cadence at the end, so we know that Va-ia will be the last two chords. The bass line has two E's an octave apart, which is a clue that a cadential 6-4 will work. We can put the ic-Va-ia figures in, remembering to sharpen the 3rd in chord V. Also, don't forget to write out 5-3 in full, because it follows a 6-4 chord.

Notice that there are two more places where the bass line is static:

In both of these cases you could use either a Ic-Va progression, or a suspension.

- The first shaded chord fits ic-Va in A minor, and the second shaded chord fits Ic-Va in the relative major key of C – it's a very brief modulation.

- Or if you prefer, each shaded chord has a dissonant interval of a 4th which falls to a consonant 3rd, so you could use the suspension figures 4-3. (Notice that 4-3 is actually part of the figure 6/4 – 5/3 anyway – the two progressions are very close).

When you've finished with the cadences and suspensions, work through the rest of the piece. Here's another bar to work through together, (the key is G minor).

The chord we are working on is shaded. We need a chord with D and A in it. The only possible chord is V. Because it's a minor key, chord V will usually be major (D major). D is the bass note, so it's root position. We need to add a # for the third.

The chord must contain C and Eb. Two chords contain these notes, C minor (iv) and A diminished (ii°). We will move on and see if the subsequent chords affect our choice.

We only have a D – it could be chord V, III or i. We will come back to this one too.

The chord must contain Eb and C. Only C minor (iv) is possible here, because the other chord with these notes in is A diminished, which is best used in first inversion. As Eb is the bass note, it must be ivb.

48

D and Bb are in chord i and chord III (Bb major). Chord i would be in 2nd inversion, so chord III is the better choice. The bass note is D, so it's first inversion. Watch out though – we've already sharpened the F's in this bar with the first accidental, so we need a natural sign to make sure that the chord is Bb major and not Bb augmented!

C and A are part of chord A dim (ii°), and F major (VII). F major would be 2nd inversion and A dim would be first – so A dim is the correct chord.

Now let's go back to the chords we missed, and write in the Roman numerals so we can see what's happening with the chord progressions.

We could choose from any of these progressions for these two chords: IV-V, ii°-V, IV-III, ii°-III. Remember to pick the most likely progression – in this case IV-V and ii°-V are common.

Since we've got ii° already at the end of the bar, IV-V will be more effective. Both are root position chords, so we just need to add a # on to chord V.

49

7. CHOOSING CHORDS – EXERCISES

Figure these bass lines appropriately. A chord change is expected with each asterisk. Begin by locating any likely cadences, (and use them to work out the key). Next, scan through looking for places where a suspension might work. Finally, add in the rest of the chords, using the most likely progressions. Leave any 5-3 chords blank, unless they are part of a 6/4- 5/3 progression or need accidentals.

1. Adapted from *Chorale 362 "Es ist gewißlich an der Zeit",* by J.S. Bach

2. Adapted from *Chorale 195 "Wie schön leuchtet der Morgenstern",* by J.S. Bach.

Take careful notice here of the key – you have a choice of keys at the first cadence, but not at the second.

3. Adapted from *Chorale 196 "Da der Herr Christ zu Tische saß",* by J.S. Bach.

Here, notice the use of both B natural and B flat – what keys are used here? In two places you are asked to provide two chords for a single bass note – think about why this might be: imagine what might be happening in the inner parts.

7. CHOOSING CHORDS – ANSWERS

Suggested answers – a range of answers are possible.

1. Notice that the cadential 6-4 in the last bar has an accented passing note in the melody – make sure you don't use two Va chords instead of Ic-Va.

2. The first cadence can be treated as iia-Va in D major or V7a-Ia in A major. In the last-but-one chord, the soprano C# should be considered an accented passing note in the E major chord.

3. This chorale switches between C minor (with B naturals) and its relative major, Eb major. The single bass notes which require two chords should alert you to places where a suspension is needed. In both cases here, the suspension will be in an inner part. In the 9-8 suspension, one of the inner parts would have F (prepared in the previous Bb major chord) falling to Eb. In the 7-6 suspension, G (prepared in the previous C minor chord) falls to F.

8. PROBLEM AREAS

In this lesson we will focus on some particularly problematic areas of figuring a bass.

ACCENTED PASSING & AUXILIARY NOTES

Sometimes the melody note directly above the bass note is **not** actually a chord note, but instead it is an **accented passing note or accented auxiliary note**. Take the shaded chord in this bar for example:

If we assume that the melody note to use in the chord is B, we need a chord with B and D: G major or B minor. Only a first inversion B minor chord is possible, as we can't use a second inversion G major chord here (it's not Ic but IVc). However, notice the C natural; the accidental should alert you to the fact that the piece is **modulating**.

The use of C natural means that the piece is changing key to G major. Remember that when a modulation occurs, the most likely chord is **V7** in the new key, so we would expect a chord of D7 at this point. Instead of using the B in the chord, we can treat it as an accented passing note, and focus on the C natural instead. This gives us two of the notes from V7a in the new key, figured with a 7 and a natural sign:

It can be tricky to spot places where an accented passing/auxiliary note occurs. Look out for key changes, and if you are ever stuck with a chord that does not seem to work, consider whether an accented passing note will fix the problem!

DECORATIVE NOTES IN THE BASS

Most of the time you only have one bass note to deal with. Sometimes however, the bass line is decorated, which you might find confusing. You might be wondering if you should count **all** the bass notes when working out the inversion, if the decoration includes chord notes. The answer is **no**. Only count the bass note directly above the asterisk.

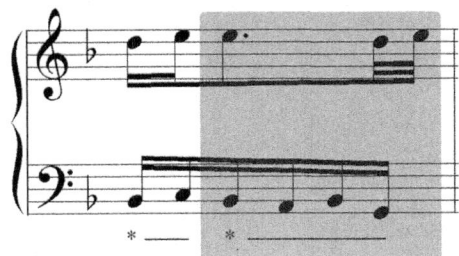

The key is F major. In the shaded box, the bass note above the asterisk is Bb, but the lowest note in the group is G. The E and Bb occur in chords vii° and V7. Chord vii°, being diminished, will usually only occur in first inversion, with G in the bass. But here the true bass note is Bb, not G. It is best considered as V7d – figured with 4/2.

Try to work out the function of each decorated note – which are part of the harmony? Here, the A is an auxiliary note, between Bb and G, so it's not part of the harmony. The G, on the other hand, is an auxiliary **harmony** note (i.e. another note in the chord) and therefore part of the harmony.

ACCIDENTAL TRAPS

Be very careful to add in all necessary accidental signs to your figures. Out of the following scenarios, points 3 and 4 are the trickiest to spot. With any bar which contains accidentals, analyse each chord carefully to make sure that the correct accidentals are present.

1. Chord V in a minor key piece is a **major chord** > raise the third of the triad.

2. An accidental given in the melody must still be shown in the figured bass.

3. A previous accidental in the **bass part** or **melody line** might need to be **cancelled** further along the bar – check!

4. A previous accidental in the **figured bass** might need to be cancelled further along the bar – check!

Here are some examples to illustrate:

1. The key is A minor. The shaded chord is the dominant, which should be E **major**. A sharp is needed in the figured bass:

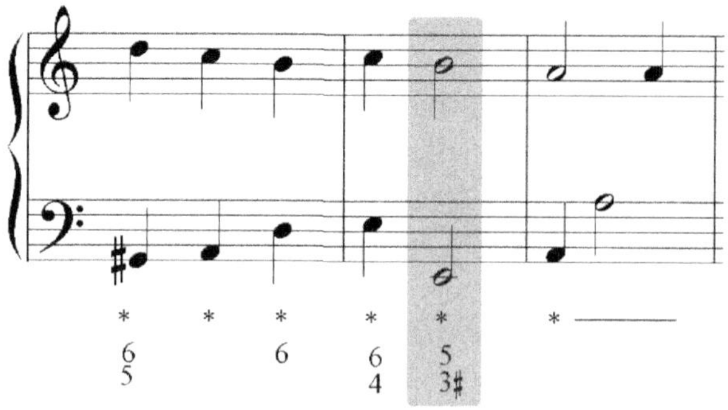

2. The sharp in the melody line has to be shown in the figured bass:

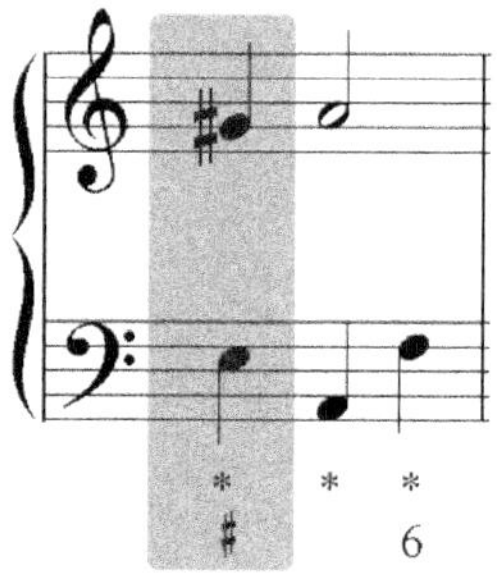

3. The F# accidental in the bass line needs to be cancelled for chord iv, which is a D **minor** chord in A minor. (It was sharpened previously as an auxiliary note to prevent an augmented 2nd G#-F in the bass line).

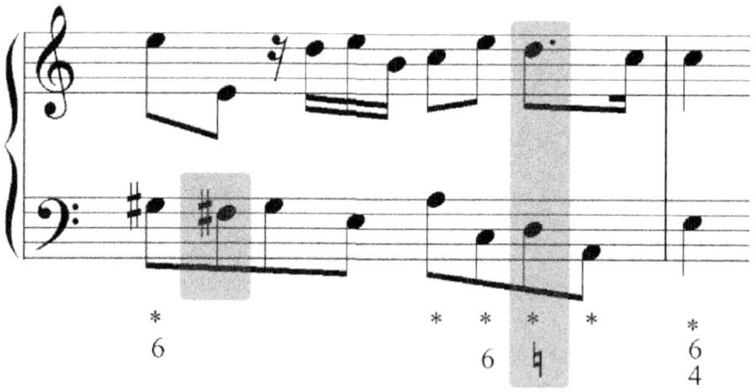

4. The G was sharpened in the figured bass at the beginning of the bar for chord V, but the shaded chord is III, which would be **augmented** if it contained G#. The natural sign is needed to make the C major chord.

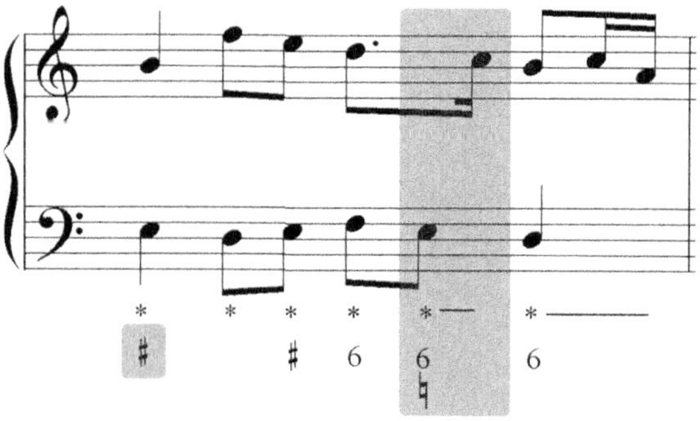

8. PROBLEM AREAS – EXERCISES

EXERCISE 1

Look at the excerpt below and answer the questions.

a. What key does the piece begin in, and what key does it modulate to?

b. In the excerpt below, circle any notes in the **soprano** part which you believe are **accented** passing or auxiliary notes.

c. Now look at the notes labelled A-D in the bass line, and say whether each one is part of the harmony or is a non-chord note.

A: C:

B: D:

EXERCISE 2

Now add a figured bass line using one chord under each asterisk. Leave 5-3 chords blank, unless they form part of a 6-4 5-3 progression or need accidentals.

8. PROBLEM AREAS – ANSWERS

EXERCISE 1

a. G major, modulating to D major.

b. See below.

c.

A: Yes   C: No

B: Yes (it's part of the added 7th chord)   D: Yes

EXERCISE 2

Note: the 6-5 and 7 chords are preferred because the added 7th is important for the modulation.

9. PRACTICE QUESTIONS

Indicate suitable chords for a continuo player by figuring the bass as necessary at the places marked * in these excerpts. 5-3 chords should be left blank, unless they are part of a 6-4 5-3 progression, or need any chromatic alteration. All other chords should be indicated, as well as any suspended dissonances (suspensions).

Each question carries a total of 15 marks. For 12-15 marks, your answer needs to meet these criteria:

- The key/tonality/modulations (if present) have been correctly perceived
- The figuring provides a musically satisfactory harmonic structure and some sense of style
- The harmonic vocabulary shows some initiative, and features such as sequences have been correctly observed

1. (Begin in bar 5)

2. (Begin in bar 2)

9. PRACTICE QUESTIONS – ANSWERS

There are several possible working for these questions. The below answers would receive full marks.

1.

2.

SECTION 2 – HARMONIC RECONSTRUCTION

1. INTRODUCTION TO THE RECONSTRUCTION QUESTION

Question two in the grade 7 music theory exam asks you to reconstruct a piece from the given harmonic outline of a real piece of music. This question usually asks you to reconstruct a **Bach chorale**, but not always. You could also find keyboard piece from the early Classical era, for example by Haydn, or even by a lesser-known composer such as Kuhlau.

Late Baroque and early Classical music followed very strict rules regarding harmony. You will remember from grade 6 that there are rules about which notes can follow each other (known as "voice-leading"), which intervals may not follow each other, and which notes in a chord must or cannot be doubled. When you write out your reconstruction, it goes without saying that you have to **obey the rules of harmony**.

On top of this, you will also be assessed on how well you convey the **style** of the era in question. Although it's impossible to reconstruct a piece of music and end up with the exact same composition that the composer wrote originally, your reconstruction should sound as though it **could have been written** by that composer in that era.

THE HARMONIC OUTLINE

If you take any piece of music and strip out the **melodic decoration**, you are left with a row of chords. Your task is to put some melodic decoration back in, so that it sounds like a real piece of music again.

Here is the beginning of Chorale no.1 from J.S. Bach's "371 Harmonized Chorales".

Here is the same piece, with the melodic decoration removed. Compare the two carefully.

You will be given an outline like this, and will attempt to make something like the first version.

TYPES OF EMBELLISHMENT

There are several kinds of melodic decoration or embellishment we can consider:

- Passing notes

- Auxiliary notes

- Suspensions

- Changing notes

- Auxiliary harmony notes

We will look at each of these in detail in the following lessons.

KEEPING IN STYLE

Look again at Chorale No.1 and its outline. Notice that:

a. *The soprano line is not altered very much.*
A chorale is hymn tune. Bach took the religious songs which were well known by the Lutheran church congregations of his day, and he harmonised them. Sometimes he harmonised the same hymn in several different ways. The important thing to understand is that the **melody** needs to remain mostly the same, otherwise the hymn would not be recognisable. A tiny bit of embellishment is all right, however.

b. *Not every chord is embellished.*
Melodic decoration has to be added with moderation. You can safely aim to embellish about 75% of the chorale. Chords with a **pause** symbol are **not decorated**.

c. *No more than two parts are decorated simultaneously.*
Actually, Bach frequently simultaneously decorated all four-parts of the harmony, but then again, he is the undisputed master of chorale harmonisation. Until you are better than Bach, it is advisable to keep most of your melodic decoration to **one part at a time**, and to decorate two simultaneous parts very rarely and with great caution.

GETTING TOP MARKS

The ABRSM awards the highest marks for reconstructions which follow the rules of harmony, keep to the correct style and which:

- Avoid clashing harmonies. Clashing harmonies are not the same as dissonances. Dissonances are governed by the rules of harmony and are encouraged, whereas clashes are just painful. (I'll explain about clashes later).

- Use rhythmic motifs consistently. You might find that the outline you have been given includes a few bars with fancy, twiddly bits using semiquavers (sixteenth notes). It is wise to include a moderate amount of your own similar embellishments, using the same rhythm.

PLAN OF ACTION

These are the steps you will need to follow. Each step is explained in detail in the next lessons.

1. Go through the piece and add some **passing notes**. (See lesson 2).

2. Go through it once more and add some **suspensions**. (See lesson 3).

3. Go through it again and add some **auxiliary notes**. (See lesson 4).

4. Go through it again and add some **changing notes.** (See lesson 5).

5. Check how many chords you have decorated. If you have done about 75%, it will be enough. If not, add some more.

6. Look carefully at the parts of the answer given by the ABRSM. If there are any unusual rhythms (i.e. something which is not a plain crotchet (quarter note) or pair of quavers (eighth notes)), make sure that the same rhythms occur in your own reconstructed part too.

7. Check one last time looking for problems, such as consecutive 5ths or clashing harmonies.

1. INTRODUCTION - EXERCISES

Answer **True** or **False** to these statements.

1. Question 2 in the grade 7 music theory exam asks you to reconstruct a piece of music from any musical era.

2. You will be given a harmonic outline, and will have to make it sound like a real piece of music.

3. It's important to show your creativity as a composer and try to use contemporary techniques.

4. It's ok to change the given chords if you think you can write something which sounds better.

5. It's a good idea to re-use some of the existing rhythms of the piece.

6. You should only use one type of melodic decoration throughout, to be consistent.

7. You don't have to decorate every chord.

8. Chords marked with a pause should not be decorated.

9. The soprano line in a chorale should be decorated as much as possible.

10. The rules of harmony don't apply in this question.

1. INTRODUCTION - ANSWERS

Answer **True** or **False** to these statements.

1.   False. It will only be from the late Baroque or early Classical era.

2.   True.

3.   False. It's important to write in the style of the piece.

4.   False. You must use the provided harmonic outline.

5.   True.

6.   False. You should use a variety of types of melodic decoration.

7.   True. Around 75-80% is a good target.

8.   True.

9.   False. The soprano line in a chorale should be decorated as **little** as possible.

10. False. The rules of harmony **do** apply in this question.

2. ADDING PASSING NOTES

WHERE TO ADD PASSING NOTES

A passing note can be added

- often between two notes which are a **third** apart

- occasionally between two notes which are a **major second** apart, as a chromatic passing note

- to the alto, tenor and bass lines, but only very rarely to the soprano line.

Scan each part, looking for a rising or falling third. (Don't forget to also look at the notes at the **end of the** stave compared to the notes starting the next one.)

Here's an example bar. (There are two falling thirds in the soprano line – but since this forms the melody, we should avoid altering it.)

The tenor part has a falling third between the A and F#. We can fill this gap with a **passing note G.**

Sometimes it is possible to fill in the gap between two notes which are a fifth apart, especially if they are minims (half notes). Two passing notes will be needed, and one extra chord note.

Here is an example. The bass line has a rising fifth. We can fill in the gaps with a chord note C (part of the A minor chord), and passing notes B and D:

Passing notes can be put into two parts at the same time (if you are brave). Together, they should make the harmonic interval of a 3rd or a 6th.

In this example, both the tenor and bass parts have rising thirds (melodic interval). The added passing notes are a third apart (harmonic interval). This is fine.

The alto and tenor have rising melodic thirds here, but the harmonic interval is a sixth. This is ok too.

TYPE OF PASSING NOTE

You will remember that there are two kinds of passing note, the **unaccented** and the **accented.**

- Unaccented passing notes fall between the chords. They are the most common type of passing note.

- Accented passing notes fall **on the beat**, pushing the chord note off the beat. They are less common.

In this case, we could use either an accented or unaccented passing note.

PROBLEMS TO CHECK FOR

After adding a passing note, you need to check that you have NOT created:

- Consecutive perfect 5ths and octaves

- Clashes caused by accidentals in other parts

- 3 to 5 at a perfect cadence

- Melodic intervals which are augmented or diminished

CONSECUTIVES

Here's an example of a forbidden consecutive caused by a passing note. Notice what happens if we insert an A between the B and the G in the alto part:

Consecutive perfect 5ths have appeared in the soprano and alto parts. This is not allowed.

CLASHES

Here's an example of a clash. The bass line rises from E to G, giving an opportunity to add a passing note.

If we simply fill in the gap with an accented passing note, we get this:

The F# in the tenor clashes with the F natural in the alto part. This should be avoided.

3 TO 5 AT A PERFECT CADENCE

At a perfect cadence, the third of chord V (e.g. B in a G major chord) is often (in the alto or tenor part) followed by the fifth of chord I (G in a C major chord). This creates a melodic gap of a third (B-G), but a passing note usually sounds pretty bad in this position. The B functions as a leading note, and should really "lead" to the tonic C. Bach often let the leading note fall to the dominant instead. If you add a passing note here, the dominant note (G) is emphasised instead of the tonic and the chord sounds odd.

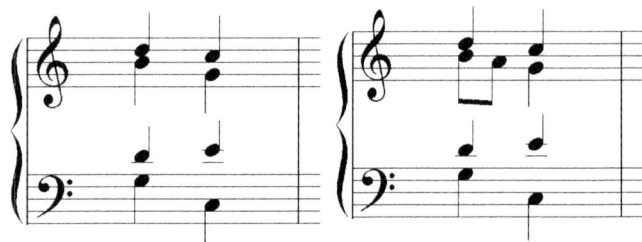

Play the two chords to hear the difference.

AUGMENTED AND DIMINISHED INTERVALS

In a minor key, take care to avoid augmented or diminished intervals. Raise a passing note by a semitone (half step) when necessary.

Here is an example in A minor. There is an opportunity for a passing note in the alto part.

If we write an F, we create a melodic interval of an augmented second (F-G#). You might like the sound of it yourself, but Bach probably wouldn't have written it! He would have raised the F up by a semitone to F#. Play both examples to understand the difference.

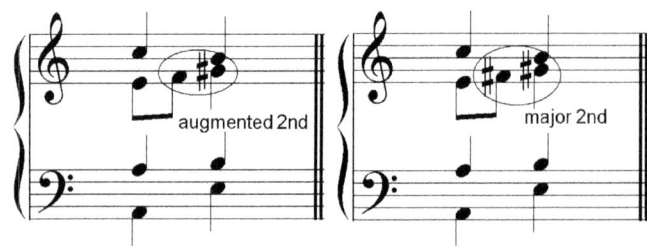

Bach did sometimes use a diminished 5th in his part-writing. However, we suggest you play it safe and avoid them.

2. PASSING NOTES - EXERCISES

EXERCISE 1

For each of the following passing notes, decide whether it is correct, or has broken a rule. If incorrect, explain which rule has been broken.

EXERCISE 2

Add one **unaccented** passing note to each of these pairs of chords, **unless doing so breaks a rule of harmony.**

EXERCISE 3

Copy these bars onto the stave below, adding one **accented** passing note to each pair.

2. PASSING NOTES - ANSWERS

EXERCISE 1

a – incorrect. There are consecutive 5ths.

b – incorrect. There is an augmented 2nd interval between the C and D#.

c – correct

d – correct

e – incorrect. The F (alto) clashes with the F# (tenor). Also, the gap between the tenor and alto parts is too wide.

EXERCISE 2

EXERCISE 3

3. ADDING SUSPENSIONS

WHAT IS A SUSPENSION?

A suspension happens when a note from a chord is held over (or repeated) in the following chord, creating a brief dissonance with the bass note. The held note then falls to a note belonging to the second chord.

Look at these two chords. The F belongs to the first chord (V7):

If the F is suspended, it becomes part of the following chord:

It then falls to E, which is the proper note to complete the C major chord.

Suspensions contain a dissonance between the **suspended note** and the **bass**. The dissonant intervals are

- the 4th
- the 7th
- the 9th

In our example, the suspended note is a 4th above the bass. (It's actually a compound 4th, but it makes no difference!)

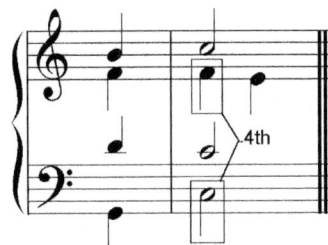

Suspensions are made up of **three parts**.

- The first is called the **preparation**. This is when we first hear the note which is going to be suspended.

preparation

- The second is the **suspension** itself. The preparation and suspension can be tied together, if you prefer.

suspension

- The last part is the **resolution**. The suspension should **fall** (not rise) to the resolution note.[1]

resolution

---

[1] Suspensions which rise are actually called "retardations". They are much less common than suspensions and can be safely avoided in this question.

WHERE TO ADD SUSPENSIONS

When you are looking for somewhere to add a suspension, you need to make sure that **all** the following criteria are met. It may sound difficult, but there are usually a few opportunities for suspensions in a chorale.

Suspensions should only be added:

1. where a voice part **falls** by an interval of a **2ⁿᵈ**

2. to the **alto** and **tenor** parts (but rarely to the soprano and not at all to the bass[2])

3. when the suspended note makes a dissonance with the bass

4. only when the suspended note is **not already** in the soprano, alto or tenor parts of the resolution chord (it's ok if the suspended note is already in the bass part of the resolution chord).

To help you remember, make a mental picture of yourself being suspended in a muddy bog. Learn the word MUD.

- M – Middle parts (alto and tenor)

- U – Unique note (not already in soprano, alto or tenor parts)

- D – Dissonant with the bass

Here's an example of how we would check the given outline for a possible place to add a suspension.

1. Scan the alto and tenor lines for **falling 2nds**.
    Here, the falling E-D is fine.

2. Check the interval formed between the **first note** and the **bass of the second chord**. It should be a dissonance (4ᵗʰ, 7ᵗʰ or 9ᵗʰ).
    In our example, it's a 9ᵗʰ.

---

[2] It is possible to create a suspension in the bass line, but the opportunities are rare, so we don't suggest it in the exam.

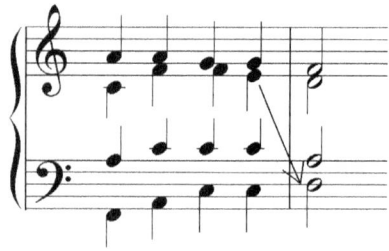

3. Make sure the **second note** doesn't exist in the other upper parts in the **second chord**, in other words, make sure it is **unique.**
   In our example, the alto D doesn't occur in the soprano or tenor parts, so that's fine.

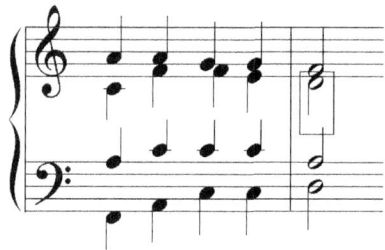

(The D does occur in the bass part, but it's only the upper parts that matter).

4. Create the suspension.

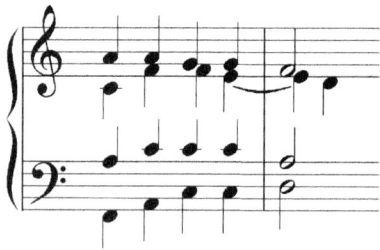

Problems to Check For

Be careful not to create clashing harmonies.

In this case, the alto part falls by a second (G-F), and the F is unique in the resolution chord. However the result would be a G natural against a G sharp, which would make a terrible clash.

3. SUSPENSIONS - EXERCISES

EXERCISE 1

Complete the paragraph about suspensions.

Suspensions can be written when two adjacent chord notes are an interval of a [a]_____ apart. The first note should create a dissonance with the bass, with the interval of a [b]_____, _____ or _____. The second note should be [c] higher/lower than the first note. The second note should [d] be/not be present in the other parts of the chord, not including the bass. Suspensions are most commonly found in the [e] soprano/alto and [f] tenor/bass parts. The three phases which make up a suspension are called the [g]_____, the suspension and the [h]_____.

EXERCISE 2

Which of these suspensions are correct? What is wrong with the incorrect suspensions?

EXERCISE 3

Find three legal places to add suspensions to the **alto** or **tenor** parts, then copy the whole piece and add the suspensions, with ties.

3. SUSPENSIONS - ANSWERS

EXERCISE 1

a) second;   b) 4th, 7th or 9th;   c) lower;   d) not be;   e) alto;   f) tenor;   g) preparation;
h) resolution.

EXERCISE 2

a) correct;   b) incorrect, the resolution note F already exists in the soprano part;
c) incorrect, the preparation note G is consonant with the bass (C), it should be dissonant;
d) correct;   e) correct

EXERCISE 3

The boxed notes show the legal suspensions.

The circled notes are not legal places for suspensions, because the resolution note already exists in an upper part of the chord (E in the first case and C in the second).

4. ADDING AUXILIARY NOTES

WHERE TO ADD AUXILIARY NOTES

An auxiliary note can be added

- between two notes which are identical

Auxiliary notes can be

- **upper or lower** (the auxiliary note is **higher** or **lower** than the chord note)

- **accented or unaccented** (the auxiliary note is **on** or **off** the beat)

- **diatonic or chromatic** (the auxiliary note is **part of the diatonic scale** or **not**).

Here are examples of each type. Imagine we have two identical Gs in our voice part, in the key of C major.

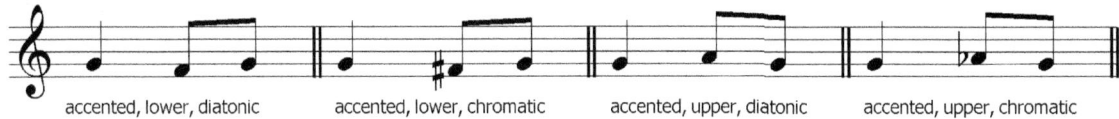

unaccented, lower, diatonic   unaccented, lower, chromatic   unaccented, upper, diatonic   unaccented, upper, chromatic

accented, lower, diatonic   accented, lower, chromatic   accented, upper, diatonic   accented, upper, chromatic

Things to look out for when writing auxiliary notes:

- Avoid augmented and diminished intervals

- Check for consecutive 5ths and octaves

- Raise the leading note in a minor key

- Stick to **diatonic** auxiliary notes for the most part, in order to keep to the correct style. However, you can often chromatically sharpen a subdominant lower auxiliary note (e.g. the F#s in our above examples). Chromatic auxiliaries are used mostly when the music modulates.

Here are some examples. The key is A minor. An auxiliary note F will make an interval of an augmented 2nd. To avoid this, we sharpen the F.

aug 2nd   maj 2nd

The addition of an upper auxiliary G here creates consecutive 5ths – this isn't allowed.

consec. 5th

A second type of auxiliary note is the "auxiliary **harmony** note". Whereas an ordinary auxiliary note forms a **dissonance** with the other notes of the chord, an auxiliary harmony note is **consonant** with the rest of the chord (i.e. it is a note which already exists in the chord). This kind of note is most often found in the **bass part**.

When to Add Auxiliary Harmony Notes

- If you are stuck and cannot find any other place to add some other melodic decoration, but need the general pace of the piece to be consistent

- When the resulting bass line is satisfactory

Here are some examples for you to play.

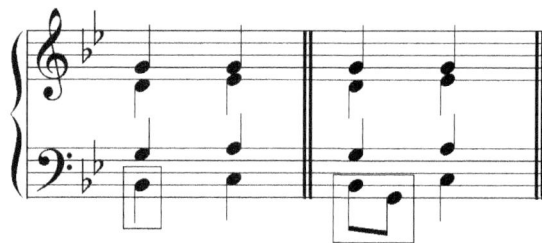

The 1ˢᵗ inversion G minor chord has an auxiliary G added to the bass line. It wasn't easy to add any other kind of melodic decoration at this point, and the G adds considerable interest to the bass line.

This time a G an octave lower is added to the root position G minor chord. This strengthens the bass line, because the lower pitched note and the rise of a perfect 5ᵗʰ are more emphatic.

As always, check for consecutives and augmented/diminished intervals!

4. AUXILIARIES - EXERCISES

EXERCISE 1

Write auxiliary notes as indicated. The key is B minor. Use diatonic auxiliaries but add any necessary

accidentals required by the minor key.

EXERCISE 2

Find 3 places to add unaccented auxiliary notes to this piece. Don't decorate any chords which have

already been decorated. Copy the piece, including the 3 new auxiliary notes, onto the stave below.

EXERCISE 3

At the places marked a-f, add either **diatonic unaccented passing notes**, or **auxiliary harmony notes**

to the **bass line**. Be careful not to introduce any consecutive 5ths or octaves!

4. AUXILIARIES - ANSWERS

EXERCISE 1

1b – raise the leading note by a semitone when it is followed by the tonic

1f – G natural is not allowed, because it would cause an augmented 2nd

EXERCISE 2

EXERCISE 3

a) fall to A would also be ok

d) leap to C is not possible, as it would create a consecutive octave with the tenor part

e) as d)

5. ADDING CHANGING NOTES

WHERE TO ADD CHANGING NOTES

Changing notes can be added between two chord notes which are **any** interval apart (except the unison, because between a unison we find the **auxiliary note**). They can be added to the alto, tenor or bass parts, but only rarely to the soprano. They are dissonant with the rest of the chord.

A changing note pattern consists of a **leap and a step in the opposition direction**. ("Step" means an interval of a 2nd, and "leap" means any interval bigger than a 2nd).

Here are some ascending melodic intervals from a second to a fifth. (It's rare to find larger melodic intervals in a chorale).

We can add a changing note which moves by **step down** from the first note, then moves by a **leap up** to the second note.

Or, we could add a changing note which moves by a **leap up**, then a **step down**.

Let's look at some descending melodic intervals in the same way:

As with other forms of decoration, check for **augmented/diminished** intervals and **consecutive 5ths and octaves**.

5. CHANGING NOTES - EXERCISES

EXERCISE 1

Answer the questions.

a. Changing notes can be added between melody notes of any interval, except which **one**?

b. Are changing notes usually **consonant** or **dissonant** with the rest of the chord?

c. Changing notes consist of what? (Choose) i) Two steps, ii) Two leaps or iii) A leap and a step

d. The two intervals created by changing notes should move how? (Choose) i) in the same direction or ii) in the opposite direction.

e. True or false? Consecutive 5ths/8ves caused by adding a changing note are allowed.

EXERCISE 2

Find and circle **six** changing notes in this piece.

5. CHANGING NOTES - ANSWERS

a.   The unison.

b.   Dissonant.

c.   A leap and a step.

d.   In the opposite direction.

e.   False.

EXERCISE 2

6. RECONSTRUCTING A CHORALE

Now that we have covered the necessary types of melodic decoration we can add to a harmonic outline, it's time to work through a real question. Part "A" is the harmonic outline and part "B" is where we are going to write our reconstruction.

1. We will write directly onto part A while we are working out the answer. When we're ready, we'll copy out the whole thing onto stave B. This means we don't mess up stave B too much with heaps of erasing!

2. Count the number of chords in the piece. Don't count chords with a pause mark, as they won't need any decoration. There are 15 chords here. Aim to decorate about 75-80% (three-quarters or a bit more). This means we should leave about three chords untouched, in this case.

3. Start with passing notes. Remember they can go in any part, but don't put many in the soprano part. Look for places where the melody line moves **by a third**.

Check for consecutives and clashes. Notice the chord at the first pause – the boxed notes are the 3 & 5 of their chords, so we should avoid putting passing notes here. Put the other passing notes in.

4. Next look for suspension opportunities. We can ignore the chords we've already decorated, and simply focus on the undecorated ones. Remember the acronym MUD – Middle parts, Unique note, Downward movement.

Add the suspensions, and tie them if you want to.

5. Now look for places to add auxiliary notes. They can be added between two identical notes. Again, ignore all the chords we've already decorated.

6. Add auxiliary **harmony** notes. Look in the bass part for places where a harmony note would create a satisfying bass line.

7. If you still have too many undecorated chords, add changing notes. Changing notes can be inserted between any two chord notes. In our exercise however, we've only got three undecorated chords left, so we can stop already!

You will be given the outline in full on one stave, with a blank stave directly underneath it, which is where you should now copy out your answer. The ABRSM kindly fills in a few beats for you here and there on the answer stave too.

- When adding decoration, make sure that all notes which sound at the same time are aligned vertically. For example, the alto F should be aligned with the third soprano G here:

- Copy the notes lightly but clearly, so that you can see them well but can also erase them easily.

- Be sure to copy all accidentals. In four-part harmony, it is good practice to write accidentals as though each line was on an **independent** stave. For example, the G# in the soprano part here should be given a sharp as well, even though there is one earlier in the bar, because the earlier sharp applies to the alto part.

Bad   Good

Play through the finished exercise to see how it sounds.

6. RECONSTRUCTING A CHORALE - EXERCISES

Exercise 1

Add melodic decoration to around 70-80% of the chords in this harmonic outline, in the style of a Bach chorale. Copy the whole piece onto the staves below.

Using this harmonic outline (A), reconstruct this (adapted) Bach chorale. Copy your answer onto the blank staves, below the outline (B).

6. RECONSTRUCTING A CHORALE – ANSWERS

There are many ways to answer these questions correctly.

EXERCISE 1

Suggested answer.

EXERCISE 2

Suggested answer.

7. RECONSTRUCTING A KEYBOARD PIECE

Most of the time, question 2 in the grade 7 music theory exam paper is based on a Baroque style Bach Chorale. He wrote hundreds of them, so there are plenty for the ABRSM to choose from! But it is certainly not guaranteed that a chorale will come up in your exam – it could be a keyboard piece by an early classical composer. What if it's not a chorale?

The main differences are that:

- A chorale is in strict four-part harmony, whereas a keyboard piece will have any number of notes sounding at the same time (usually between 1 and 4).

- In a keyboard piece, the rules of voice-leading are more relaxed (but not abandoned!) Augmented and diminished intervals are acceptable as long as they are treated correctly. (More on this later in the lesson.)

- In a chorale, the rhythm is usually driven by a quaver (eighth note) pulse, with a few crotchet and minim chords (quarter note and half notes). In a keyboard piece, the rhythm is likely to be very varied, with certain rhythmic "motifs" (short fragments) giving the piece its character.

- At first sight, it might seem more difficult to reconstruct a keyboard piece, as you may have difficulty knowing where to start. In actual fact, early classical composers mostly stuck to the same rules of harmony as Bach, and the differences lie in how they treat rhythm and melody.

The first step is to **analyse what you've got**. You will always be given a few bars to get you started. Don't just make a blind stab at it – look carefully at the given reconstruction and **write down what you discover.** Then, keep going in the same way. (Did that sound too easy? It's not as hard as you think!)

You will need to analyse three things:

1. The harmony   2. The melody   3. The rhythm

Let's take a look at the first two bars of the Rondo movement of Mozart's third piano sonata, composed in 1777. (The original uses appoggiaturas which have been written out in full here).

Here is the harmonic outline:

How do we get from the **outline** to the **keyboard piece?**

To understand what Mozart's harmonic plan is, we should figure out what **chords** he's using. We can start by looking at the chord names.

G7   Cm   F7   Bb

Next, look at the likely **relationships** of these chords, based on key. Remember that in Baroque/Classical music, the tonic/dominant relationship is the strongest. Here for example, G(7) is the dominant of C minor, and F(7) is the dominant of Bb major. Notice the inversions too.

G7   Cm   F7   Bb
(C minor) V7b   ia (Bb major)V7b   la

Here's the rest of the outline. Continue analysing the rest of the harmony in the outline, paying attention to any **repeating patterns.**

V7b   ia   V7b   la   Ib   IVa   Ib   Vc   la   Va   V7b   ia   V7b   la
(C minor)   (Bb major)   (C minor)   (Bb major)

Here, we can see that only primary chords are used (I, V and IV), and that the V7-I pattern from the beginning recurs from bar 4.

THE MELODY

As you know, melody is simply chord notes plus melodic decoration. We now need to work out what kind of melodic decoration has been used in the given reconstruction, so that we can continue in a similar way. The "extra notes" have been boxed; look at each note and decide what kind of decoration it is.

1. Harmonic auxiliary note (part of the G7 chord)

2. Accented passing note (between G and Eb)

3. Accented passing note (between Eb and C)

4. Harmonic auxiliary note (part of the Cm chord)

5. Harmonic auxiliary note (part of the F7 chord)

6. Accented passing note (between F and D)

7. Accented passing note (between D and Bb)

8. Harmonic auxiliary note (part of the Bb major chord)

In fact, Mozart has only used two types of melodic decoration to make this melody. These are the types of melodic decoration we should add to the rest of the outline.

Look at the **texture** – how many notes are played in each hand? In this piece, the melody is a single musical line, and the left-hand has two-note chords.

THE RHYTHM

Lastly, we need to look carefully at the note values used in the given reconstruction, including the use of rests. Also notice what **isn't there!**

*   Notice how the left-hand piano part starts with a rest, and this rhythm is repeated in the following bar.

*   The right hand uses simple note values (there are **no dotted notes, no syncopation, no very fast notes**)

RECONSTRUCTING

We're now ready to have a go at reconstructing the whole extract. To recap, we are going to continue by using:

- Harmonic auxiliary notes and accented passing notes

- A single melody line in the right hand against 2-note chords in the left hand

- A rhythm pattern including a rest in the left hand

- The same note values as in the example opening

1. The boxed area is our first beat to work on. We can do the left hand quite easily – a rest followed by the chord notes (in the same way as the given opening). For the right hand, we could think about adding a G auxiliary note, but we should compare the harmonic outlines to see how this affects the harmony. In the anacrusis bar, we've got a V7 chord and both the F and G in the right hand are therefore **chord notes**.

   However, this time the chord is Ib, so a G would be a **non-chord note**. A non-chord note would be all right, but if we want to make a stronger connection with the previous section, perhaps a chord-note would be better. We could add an auxiliary harmony note Bb, instead.

2. The next two beats are highlighted here. Because the melody has risen up to Bb, we have an ideal opportunity to use A as the next melody note, which is of course an accented passing note. We can use two-note crotchet (quarter-note) chords in the left hand.

3. We can continue in exactly the same way for the next two chords.

4. And for the end of the phrase, again we use an accented passing note, but with a crotchet (quarter note) beat.

5. For the second half of the piece, the outline texture is different, with only single notes given in the left hand. You can interpret this in a number of ways – perhaps this section is much quieter, or perhaps the left-hand notes are doubled at the octave to create a stronger mood. The right hand outline melody is the same as the opening. Clearly we need this section to be "almost the same", as the opening, with some noticeable differences. We will make it "the same but more".

Here is the outline again for reference.

To achieve "the same but more", we're going to add a **little** more melodic decoration than before, and double up the left hand.

We used a combination of auxiliary notes and passing notes and introduced some chromatics. However the harmony is **still the same** and the patterns we used are **consistent with each other**. The two highlighted areas, showing beats 3 and 4, use the same pattern:

And these two boxed areas, showing beats 1 and 2, use the same melodic pattern in **retrograde** (i.e. back-to-front).

7. RECONSTRUCTING A KEYBOARD PIECE - EXERCISES

EXERCISE 1

Look at the given harmonic outline (stave A) which is from a Haydn piano sonata, and answer the questions.

a)   What clefs are used in the left hand of the piece?

b)   What aspects of the original piece (given at the beginning of stave B) should be utilised elsewhere in the piece? Consider the type of melodic decoration used, and rhythmic or melodic elements.

c)   Continue the reconstruction on stave B.

7. RECONSTRUCTING A KEYBOARD PIECE ANSWERS

1a) The piece starts with the treble clef in the left hand, then changes to bass clef at the beginning of the second stave.

1b) The original uses auxiliary harmony notes in bar 1, and a suspension on the first beat of bar 2. Rhythmically, there is a triplet figure in the right hand, and the left hand has a minim + crotchet figure (half note + quarter note).

1c) (Suggested answer)

SECTION 3 – COMPOSITION

1. COMPOSITION QUESTION TYPES

In the ABRSM grade 7 music theory exam, there is a choice of compositions, but the type of question is different in each case. The questions are always numbered as 3a and 3b, so that's what I'll be using to refer to the different question types throughout this course.

Question 3a asks you to complete the solo part to fit a given piano accompaniment. Normally you'll be asked to complete about two full staves-worth, and you'll be given about 2-4 bars of the solo part to start you off.

The idea behind this question is that you are being tested on:

- your ability to understand the harmonic structure from the piano part, and
- your ability to create a melody which fits nicely with that accompaniment.

Typical 3a Composition

Generally, the composers used for this question are from the late classical to Romantic eras.

You don't need to add any performance directions when you do this question, and phrase marks are drawn over the staves for you, to help you figure out the melodic structure. You don't need to stick to the suggested phrase lengths, but remember, they are there to help! You are not given a choice of instrument for this question, but you can expect it to be a normal standard orchestral instrument. Your melody needs to be written at concert pitch.

Question 3b is completely different - there is no given piano accompaniment, and the style of the composition is normally much more modern than in question 3a. You are given 1 or 2 bars as a given opening for a solo instrument, with a choice of two instruments. If you choose this question, you will need to add performance directions. Your piece should be at least 8 bars long, and although the question doesn't stipulate that you need to include any modulation, you should if you want to achieve top marks. As with question 3a, you need to stick to the style of the given opening.

Occasionally in this question, you are also given a harmonic progression to work from - a series of chords written out, showing you which bars they should fall in. In this type of question, you'll also be given an opening of 1 to 2 bars, but whether you choose to use it or not is up to you.

The melody you write will need to fit the chords which are shown in the progression, with the addition of non-harmony notes, like passing notes or chromatic alterations, added in to make the tune more musical.

WHICH QUESTION SHOULD YOU CHOOSE?

Many students choose question 3b, especially when there is no chord progression given, because at first sight it seems like the easier option. Since there is no piano part that you have to fit your melody to, it can seem as though there is less you can get wrong.

In actual fact though, the ABRSM has said that candidates who choose question 3a tend to get better marks. In 3a, the structure is already made for you, whereas in question 3b, you need to make a structure yourself, and many students fail to achieve this. Although 3b gives you a lot more freedom, sometimes it's difficult to know what to do with that freedom. Really, the best thing to do is to have a go at a few practice questions of both types, to see which you manage with best.

2. MARKING CRITERIA

See http://www.abrsm.org/en/our-exams/information-and-regulations/music-theory-marking-criteria-grades-6-8/ for full details about how the ABRSM marks this question.

For question 3a, you need to have good musical grammar - this means observing the rules which you learned about when studying harmony for grade 6, and includes things like avoiding obvious consecutives and doubling the appropriate note of the harmony. You'll find details about this in the chapter on "3a Grammatical Aspects".

You also need to make sure, of course, that the solo part actually fits together properly with the piano part.

For question 3b you need to make sure you add performance directions, and they need to be meaningful ones! You need to use the ideas from the given opening or chord progressions, if you were asked to do that specifically.

There are 20 points available for the composition question, and you'll get awarded a minimum of 7 points for handing in a complete attempt at the composition, so make sure you do put something down on the page, even if you're having a really bad day.

In the ABRSM's book Music Theory in Practice, they write that "you will be assessed on your ability to produce a stylish and coherent solo part that fits the keyboard accompaniment" for question 3a. It's worth noting here that "stylish" really means "in the correct style", rather than "fancy" or "chic"!

3. SHAPE AND DIRECTION

SHAPE

To get top marks for your composition, you need to make sure that it has a good shape and a good direction, but you might not be 100% clear about what that actually means.

- If your melody moves up and down by step, you'll produce smooth slopes, going up or down.
- If your melody moves by leaps, you'll make something that looks a bit like the Himalayas.

What you need to aim for is smooth slopes, but with some leaps here and there for added interest.

To achieve this, you'll generally be making your melody move by step, with some larger leaps, and you also need to make sure that nice wide range of notes is used. A good rule of thumb would be to make sure your melody sits within a range which is wider than one octave, if at all possible.

DIRECTION

Direction is closely connected to shape. If your melody generally climbs or falls gently because you use stepwise movements for the most part, then your melody will feel like it's going somewhere, but do make sure that you're not just going up and down, and up and down, on the spot!

If your melody uses too many leaps, it will sound very jagged and spiky. Too many leaps spoils the direction of a piece of music, because you can't be sure where the melody is going - it should be going along, rather than up and down.

The harmonic structure of a piece will also help to give it direction. In question 3a and sometimes in 3b, the harmonic structure is already in place, so that's one less thing you need to worry about. Sometimes for question 3b though there is no harmonic structure outlined, so you'll need to make sure that the chord progressions which underpin your melody are actually going somewhere. I'll talk about that in more detail in the section for specifics on question 3b later in the course. For question 3b, you also need to organise your musical ideas into phrases, which is another aspect of shape.

Whichever composition you choose, try to think of the direction as being something like the plot of a story. Each musical phrase is a separate but connected part of the overall story, and you should be working towards some kind of climax, most likely just before the end of the piece.

In question 3a, there will be clues as to where the climax is anticipated - clues can be that the dynamics are increasing, that the tempo or note values used are getting faster, and that the overall range of notes at that point are of a higher pitch than elsewhere.

4. SUITABILITY TO THE INSTRUMENT

You need to make sure that the composition you write is suitable for the instrument you're writing for. Most importantly perhaps, this means you need to know what the lowest playable note on each of the standard orchestral instruments is. You really only need to be aware of the lowest playable note and not the highest, because the lowest note is defined by the size of the instrument itself, whereas the highest note depends on the player's ability. If you are not sure what the lowest note is, you can stay safe by only going as low as one ledger line below the stave, but do remember that the lowest note on the flute is middle C.

For question 3b, you also need to be aware of how articulation, (slurs or other types of attack), are a necessary part of the music.

And for both question options, it's vital to know what the instrument actually sounds like, of course, and it's useful to know roughly which part of the instrument's range produces the most expressive and flexible sounds.

THE STRING SECTION

In the string section, the violin's lowest note is G below the stave, the viola's lowest note is C below the stave, the cello's is also C, but below the bass clef stave, and the double bass's lowest note is E below the bass clef stave. Don't forget though, that the double bass is actually a transposing instrument, and its music is written an octave higher than it actually sounds.

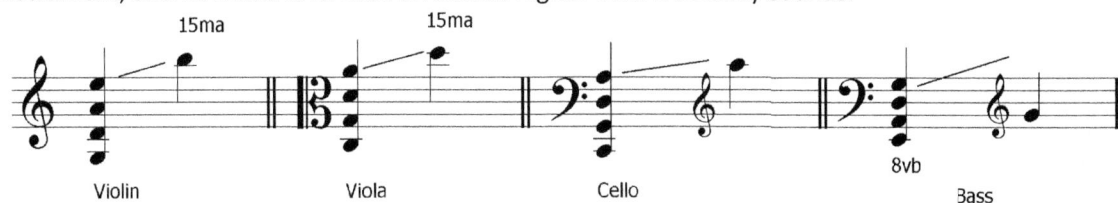

Violin   Viola   Cello   Bass

It can help to remember that the notes on each instrument form a chord of C major (G-C-C-E), but you'll need to try to memorise which note belongs to which instrument. All the string instruments have very wide playable ranges, but it's probably best to avoid adding a large number of notes with ledger lines. Stay within the stave or up to three ledgers lines maximum, so you don't make any slips in the notes you're writing.

The string instruments have more possible sounds than any other family in the orchestra. A string player can attack the instrument with either side of the bow, with their fingers, they can add mutes, and it's possible to play some chords with a technique called double or triple stopping. If you are a string player, you might want to think about adding specialist string performance directions in question 3b, such as bow directions, pizzicato and so on. But it's not a requirement at all, and you should only attempt to put specialist directions into your composition if you really know what you're doing.

There is no requirement to add even basic up and down bow markings for string instruments. Bowing directions are normally worked out logically by the player - for instance an up beat is attacked with an up bow, and so on, so there is only a need to add specific bowing instructions if you want to achieve a special effect.

The woodwind section contains the flute, oboe, clarinet and bassoon. The flute's lowest note is middle C, the oboe has Bb below the stave in the treble clef, and the bassoon has Bb below the stave in the bass clef.

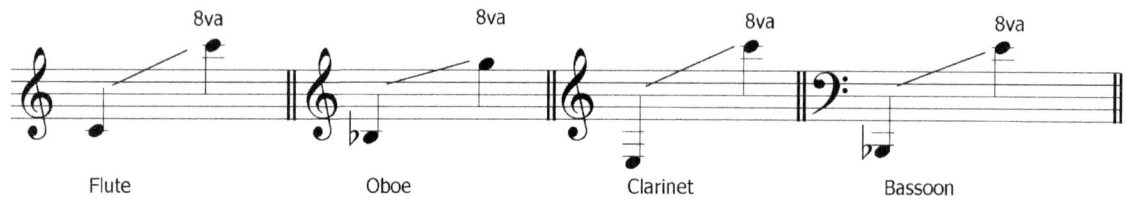

Flute · Oboe · Clarinet · Bassoon

The clarinet is a transposing instrument, but you'll be writing at concert pitch. For the clarinet, the lowest written note is E below the stave. But at concert pitch, the actual sounding lowest note is D on a Bb clarinet, or Db/C# on an A clarinet.

When you write for a woodwind instrument, it's good to know that a smaller part of the instrument's range will produce the most expressive and flexible notes. By "flexible", I mean that they have a wide dynamic range, without the sound being distorted, for example.

If you take the flute for instance, the lowest notes on the flute sound very mellow, soft and breathy, and it's pretty hard to play them at a very loud dynamic. The higher octaves on the flute produce a much brighter, and louder, sound.

The composer Rimsky-Korsakov wrote a well-respected book about orchestration, "The Principles of Orchestration", and he included a table with the sweet spot of each instrument's range. In simple terms, the most expressive range for each wind instrument begins around an octave above its lowest note, and extends for about an octave and a half.

So in other words, although the flute can play from middle C up to about C with 5 ledger lines above the stave, the optimum range will be from about the D which is a 9th above middle C, up to high G.

This doesn't mean that you can't use the lower notes of course, but it does mean you should take care not to base the whole melody around the lower end of the spectrum, and to think carefully about which dynamics would work on those less expressive notes.

ACOUSTIC CONSIDERATIONS

Next we'll take a quick look at some acoustic differences which can have an impact on how you write for a specific instrument. The flute, oboe and bassoon all overblow by an octave. This means that in order to sound out the note an octave higher than a lower note, you blow a bit harder but keep the basic finger pattern the same.

For example, a G on a flute is played with 3 fingers and the thumb, and G an octave higher is pretty much the same. This means that writing an octave leap is very effective and easy to achieve on these instruments.

On the clarinet however, things are different. The clarinet overblows by a compound perfect 5th. If you put three fingers and a thumb down on the clarinet, you produce a C, and if you blow a bit harder you sound out a G. What this means is that octave leaps are actually quite tricky. There are plenty of studies for poor clarinettists to practise the skill, but even so, you'd be better off writing leaps of a perfect 12th to be played with a good effect on the clarinet.

THE BRASS SECTION

The lowest written notes on the brass family instruments are F# below middle C on the Bb trumpet, C an octave below middle C on the horn in F, E two octaves below middle C on the trombone, and Eb two octaves below middle C on the tuba. It's actually pretty rare to get a melody for tuba or trombone in the exam, but you never know!

Trumpet   French Horn   Trombone   Tuba

Like the woodwind instruments, the very lowest notes on the instruments can be a bit poor in tone colour and difficult to play at certain dynamics, so for best results keep your melody above the lowest five or so notes.

All the brass instruments are good at crescendos and diminuendos and can easily change smoothly from pp to ff and vice versa. Overall the brass section is a little bit less capable of expressive playing than the woodwinds, (according to Rimsky-Korsakov at least!) but they can still produce a lot of expression.

With all the instruments I've mentioned, you need to add articulation when writing a melody for question 3b. Usually this is in the form of **slurs**.

For string instruments, slurred notes are played with one sweep of the bow in the same direction. It's generally not possible to play a large number of notes with one bow sweep though, so only slur smaller groups of notes - around one or two beats worth would be a good plan.

For wind and brass, slurred notes are played without any further intake of breath, and the first note is attacked with the tongue and the other notes follow in the same breath. So it goes without saying that you need to remember that the players have to breathe somewhere.

Attacking a note with the tongue or bow produces an accented effect, so avoid writing several tongued or bowed notes in a row, unless that is the effect you really want. In any case, if you did want that effect, I'd suggest putting a specific articulation on the note, such as staccato, tenuto or accents, because leaving a large number of notes with no articulation creates music that isn't easily grouped into phrases.

For the string instruments, you also need to know the tunings of the individual strings, as this is sometimes tested in questions 4 and 5 in the exam. For the wind and brass, you'll generally be safe if you avoid going any further down than one ledger line below the stave, and remember to keep the melody basically ON the stave, or up to two ledger lines above it.

5. MELODIC STRUCTURE

If you are working with a given opening, you'll need to gather some information about how that opening is **constructed**, and use **similar** ideas in the rest of your composition.

In question 3a you'll always be given a couple of bars or so to get you started.

In question 3b, you'll also be provided with an opening phrase, but if you also have a chord progression to work with, the printed opening will be optional. But even if you choose to start the composition in your own way, it needs to be carefully structured so that whatever you write at the start is related melodically to what you write further on.

TYPES OF MELODIC MOTION

There are two basic types of motion, called **conjunct** and **disjunct**. Basically these two words mean "joined together" and "not joined together". Conjunct motion is when the melody moves by step, and disjunct is when it moves by a leap of any size, from a 3rd or greater.

In most music, both types of movement are used, but there is usually more conjunct, or stepwise motion, than disjunct, within an individual tune. Conjunct motion sounds fluid and songlike and you can use quite long stretches of it at a time. Conjunct motion, in contrast, sounds more jagged or spiky and is best used in small doses.

Here are some tunes written by Mendelssohn in his collection of "Songs without Words". These pieces are written for solo piano, but their style is of a songlike melody with an accompaniment. I've isolated just the tune parts of the first few songs.

Song without Words No.1

Notice here that there are three phrases marked out: two short phrases followed by a long one which is about twice as long. The first two phrases move smoothly by step, and the only disjunct motion is between these two phrases, when the E leaps up an octave. The third phrase contains a little disjunct motion combined with conjunct - this makes the melody a bit more interesting than if it had contained only more conjunct motion.

Song without Words No.2

Again, notice how much more conjunct motion there is compared to disjunct, and that the leaps are often seen when a new phrase begins.

Song without Words No.3

Mendelssohn's third Song contains hardly any disjunct motion here, and there are also quite a lot of repeated notes. It's worth noticing though, that repeated notes tend to be used in a **rhythmic** way - notice the use of the staccato, sforzando and accents - these different articulations ensure that a repeated note has some added interest.

It's worth looking at the precise intervals used in any disjunct motion - such as the octave leap at the beginning of Mendelssohn's first "Song without Words". It can be quite effective to reuse the same interval at other places in your composition, without overdoing it of course. If the opening of your piece contains a leap of a 6th for example, it would be a good idea to incorporate the same interval in a few other places as well.

SEQUENCES

Sequences are small fragments of melody which are repeated, but starting on a different step of the scale. Sequences are a really important piece of the melodic puzzle - if you don't make any attempt to use sequences, your melody is likely to sound very random. Sequences are part of the glue that sticks the various parts of your composition together to make a coherent piece.

Look again at Mendelssohn's first "Song without Words":

At first glance you can easily see that the 2nd phrase is a sequence of the first - we have four descending conjunct notes, first beginning on A, then on E. The third phrase looks completely different, doesn't it? But if you look a little closer at the end of the third phrase you'll see that it ends with the same four-note descending pattern, and overall it descends from C# to F#. So although the rhythm is different here, it's still closely connected in terms of melody.

In the second song you can see again that sequences have been used. Bar 2 is connected to bar 1, and bars 4, 5 and 6 are similar to each other as well.

In the third song we have three repeated notes followed by three ascending conjunct notes, then the same again. In bar 3, we find the repeated As are followed by three descending notes. This is an inverted sequence - it's not an exact copy, as the rhythm is different, but you can see easily how it's related to what's gone on before. An inverted sequence simply means that the melody has been turned upside down.

So to sum up, when you write your melody, pay attention to the type of motion, and use disjunct motion with care.

Make sure that you sequence the ideas from the opening of the composition, so that your piece feels like it's glued together properly. In question 3a, you can also look at sequences ideas from elsewhere in the piano part.

6. RHYTHMIC STRUCTURE

You need to think about the rhythms that are used in your composition in pretty much the same way that you think about melody - ideas that are presented at the beginning of the piece, or in the piano accompaniment for question 3a, should be **reused** elsewhere in the rest of your piece. While you definitely don't want to just repeat the same rhythm throughout, you do need to make sure that there is a consistency within the rhythms that you use.

Take a look at the first couple of bars or so of the composition - whether they are provided for you, or you actually wrote them yourself (as is sometimes possible in question 3b).

Try to decide which of the note values seem to give the melody its **character** - usually this means looking for the most interesting or unusual bits of the rhythm.

Here's an opening which was written by Brahms - it's the beginning of the second movement of his first clarinet sonata.

What sort of rhythms has Brahms used here?

The first bar contains a long note which is repeated as a short note, then the second bar contains a tied note and a bunch of demisemiquavers or 32nd notes. These are the sort of rhythms then, that we'd expect to find re-used in the rest of the piece. They give the melody a definite shape, and you'd need to continue by using the same shapes as you go along - with some variation of course, - you don't want to it to get boring.

As you can see, the next two bars are a sequence of the first two in terms of melody and rhythm - the rhythm is identical. Bar 5 has something a little different - the tied note is in a different position here. Brahms doesn't just keep on repeating the same two-bar rhythm, but the rhythm here is clearly taken from the opening, as he's reused the demisemiquavers or 32nd notes.

What sort of note values could be considered interesting enough to give a piece character? It will very much depend on the individual piece, but some things you can look out for are:

Very quick notes

Syncopation

Dotted notes

Tied notes

Triplets

You also need to think about how rhythm works within a phrase. In question 3a, the phrases will be marked out for you, but in 3b you'll need to figure them out for yourself. The important thing to remember is that at the end of a phrase, we normally expect some kind of **cadence** - imperfect, plagal, interrupted or perfect, and a cadence forms a natural pause in the music.

In terms of rhythm, a cadence is normally signified by the use of a longish note value - usually worth at least one beat of the bar, sometimes much more.

Look again at the Brahms piece from earlier. Notice how Brahms continues his clarinet sonata - with a few bars of quavers (or eighth notes).

Andante un poco adagio

This provides a contrasting phrase with the first 6 bars, and Brahms goes on to reuse the rhythms from both of these phrases in the rest of the movement.

Look at how the section ends - on a crotchet (or quarter note F), and a rest. The longer note F helps to show that the end of a phrase or section has been reached, and the rest does the same, but also allows the player somewhere to breathe properly. Although a wind or brass player can grab quick breaths in between slurred groups of notes, it's also important to include places where a proper breath can be taken. So rests are important and have a clear function, but don't over-use them. The examiner doesn't want to see a composition that resembles John Cage's '4"33' (four minutes thirty-three seconds of silence!)

7. TIPS FOR WRITING GOOD MELODIES

As I mentioned in the lesson on shape and direction, generally you need to move by step more than by leap, and use a wide range of notes. But there is a bit more to writing a brilliant melody than just those two points of course. Here are some tips!

1. AVOID TWO LEAPS IN THE SAME DIRECTION, UNLESS THE NOTES FORM A TRIAD.

Take a look at this melody, which leaps from C to G then to D before falling back to E. It sounds pretty unmusical, almost like a random bunch of notes really.

Let's remove the double leap, and see what happens.

When the double leap is taken out, it sounds much better.

It's ok to have a double leap when all three notes (or even 4) form the notes of a recognisable chord though.

In this case, E, G, C, D sounds perfectly ok, because E, G and C make up a chord of C major.

2. AVOID LEAPS OF A 7TH

In the melody we just looked at, another reason why it sounded a bit rubbish was the fall of a 7th. It's usually better to avoiding using falls or leaps of either a major or minor 7th at all, unless they are part of the given opening, in which case you'll have to, in order to preserve the character of the piece.

A minor 7th can occasionally be used to good effect, if it is used intentionally in a V7 chord, e.g. using G-F in C major. The 7th (F) should fall by step (to E).

You can also use a diminished 7th interval, as long as you use it properly, which brings us on to point number 3.

3. IF YOU USE A DIMINISHED INTERVAL, MAKE SURE IT RESOLVES BY STEP.

Here, the notes B to F make an interval of a diminished 5th. Diminished intervals have a very unstable sound, and they have a strong pull towards a resolution, usually the nearest possible note. B to F is best resolved by moving to E - the semitone away from F.

If you swapped the melody notes around, the interval would still be a diminished 5th, but the B needs to resolve to C instead.

Here's an example of a diminished interval which hasn't been resolved. Notice how it sounds much more awkward.

4. AUGMENTED INTERVALS CAN ALSO BE USED, BUT USE THEM WITH CARE!

An augmented interval is an inverted diminished interval. Augmented intervals generally sound ok if they are the two notes from a dominant 7th chord. For example, in C major the dominant 7th chord is G7, G-B-D-F. Moving from B down to F creates an augmented 4th. As with diminished intervals, you can use this dissonance, as long as you make sure that the dissonance is resolved to the nearest note: here for example, F moves to E.

Other augmented intervals, that are not found within the dominant 7th chord, such as augmented 2nds, are best avoided, unless you can hear the melody in your head clearly and are 100% certain that it sounds ok.

5. LEADING NOTE LEADS TO THE TONIC.

Whenever you write a leading note, or 7th degree of the scale, keep a close eye on what's going on with the harmony. If the harmony is V moving to I, then your leading note will preferably lead to the tonic in the next chord. Here, the key is A minor, and G# is the leading note, so it should be followed by A. Avoid "leading" to the tonic an octave higher or lower – this usually sounds awkward.

You can always decorate the leading note of course, for example with an auxiliary note.

6. END ON THE TONIC

Your melody needs to end on the tonic note in whatever key you've arrived at. Although you might think that a mediant or a dominant note might produce a nice effect, the examiner might not agree with you! A tonic note is always correct.

7. CADENCES ARE PAUSES

Whenever there is a cadence or end of phrase, the music will have a natural pause. Make sure that this is reflected in your melody by using longer note values at the end of a phrase.

Alternatively, or perhaps in addition, you can add rests at the end of phrases - this is always appreciate by wind and brass players who often suffer from not being given anywhere to breathe.

8. QUESTION 3A – GRAMMATICAL ASPECTS

In question 3a, you are expected to get the grammatical aspects of your composition mostly correct.

The definition of the word grammar could be "a set of structural rules governing composition". In language, this means things like rules about how plurals and tenses are formed, and in music, it relates to the rules you've already come across which apply to harmony.

What you need to understand is that the rules were laid down many years ago - hundreds of years ago, in fact, and they are actually a description of the practice at that time, as decided by a small group of music theorists who thought they knew best. Whether they did or they didn't isn't important - what's important to know is that the rules are **descriptive** and not prescriptive.

In other words, these rules explain how to achieve a particular end - music that conforms to the ideals of the **classical and early Romantic** eras.

It doesn't mean that you have to follow these rules in everything you do. If you are composing for yourself, rather than in an exam situation, it's completely up to you whether you choose to break the rules or not, and no one is going to arrest you. Plenty of successful composers actually became successful because they chose to break some of these rules - Debussy loved consecutive 5ths, and Schoenberg decided that he didn't even agree with the diatonic scale system. In real life, you can let your creativity go wild.

But in an exam situation, in specifically in this exam, you're being tested on your ability to write something in the **correct style**, which means observing the rules that composers generally DID observe in the 18th and 19th centuries.

Here are some of the things you need to look out for.

CONSECUTIVES

You want to avoid creating a melody that moves in **consecutive perfect 5ths or octaves** with any part of the accompaniment. Look at the left hand piano part as well as the right hand.

In this example, if we followed the Bb in the melody part with an A, we'd be creating consecutive octaves with the right hand piano part.

You're less likely to write a consecutive if your melody moves in contrary motion, but when you're trying to fit it against two parts, it's often the case that it will be moving in similar motion, or in other words, in the same direction as one of the piano staves, so look carefully.

The rules about consecutives are not quite as strict as they are when you write 4-part harmony though. Occasionally, they could be used for a special effect - think of the beginning of Beethoven's famous 5th symphony, where the entire orchestra plays in unison.

Consecutives could also work well at a strong perfect cadence, for example. They will also be allowable if they are used in the given opening in some way, and you use them in a similar way. The point is that you should be aware of what's going on. Don't let a consecutive creep in unobserved - if they are there, they should be there for a very good reason.

DOUBLING

Generally speaking, it's always going to be ok to double up the bass note of a chord. The only exception to this is if the bass note is the **leading note**, which should never be doubled when V moves to I.

Here for example, you might be tempted to follow the E with a D#, but as there's already a D# in the accompaniment, and D# is the leading note in E minor, it would be better to pick, for example, a B instead.

The reasoning behind this is, that the leading note has a very strong pull towards the tonic, and should generally be followed by the tonic note. If you put two leading notes into a chord, you will have two pulls towards the tonic, but you have to avoid consecutive octaves, so you'll come unstuck.

Generally speaking, it's ok to double the root or 5th in any chord.

The note which you should never double without thinking it through carefully, is the **3rd** of the triad. In a diminished chord, the 3rd is usually the best note to double, but in all other chords it's usually the least satisfactory. In a major root position chord it usually has a much better effect when it's NOT doubled, so that is definitely one to avoid.

OMISSIONS

A chord without a root is slightly ambiguous. If you hear an E and a G, you could interpret them as belonging to a chord of C major, or E minor. But as it's the root note which gives a triad its foundation, our brains tend to process a two-note harmony as a root and a third, so E-G will be heard as E minor.

If you intended C major at that point, you're likely to confuse the listener. So, never miss out the root.

The 5th on the other hand can be missed out without causing any problems.

The 3rd should never be missed out - it's the note which makes the difference between a major and minor chord. This "empty" chord with no third sounds peculiar – it is reminiscent of medieval music.

The 3rd and root don't need to sound **immediately** in each chord. You can have a harmony begin with an incomplete chord, where the root or third are sounded slightly later. The strange chord in the previous example sounds fine here, with the addition of an E just afterwards.

Make sure that the root and third do appear at some point before the harmony changes again.

When you're composing, it's best to keep an eye on the grammatical aspects as you go along. Don't attempt to compose something, then go back and check it for errors, because if you do, and you do find a mistake, you'll end up at square one. Instead, it's much better to check what you're writing as you put down each note. It's a bit time consuming at first, but with a bit of practice it'll soon become second nature.

SUSPENSIONS

Another thing to watch out for is suspensions. A suspension happens when a note from one chord is held over or delayed, when the following chord sounds, producing a momentary dissonance. It normally resolves by step downwards to a chord note. The effect of the dissonance is produced by the tension set up by **delaying** the real chord note, so it's important not to spoil the "punchline" by adding the resolution note **too soon**. Here's an example of what I mean:

Looking only at the solo part, it seems natural to write a C as the note after D, but it would be a bad idea, because it will ruin the tension of the suspension. Here the right hand piano D is suspended and resolves to C, so C is the note which is delayed in order to create tension. If you write a C as the first note in this bar, the suspension will be overridden - you won't even notice it. In this situation, the best note will be G. We can't write an Eb because it would cause consecutive octaves.

TYPES OF MOTION

Similar motion is when the parts move in the same up/down direction as each other.

Contrary motion is when they move in opposite directions.

And oblique motion is when one part stays still, and the other moves.

You need to aim for contrary and oblique motion for the vast majority of the time, as this will help to create independent parts and avoid consecutives. Because you're writing a piece on 3 staves, you'll mostly likely have a lot of similar motion between two of the parts, and that's ok, so long as you use contrary motion in the other part.

What you want to avoid is all three parts moving in similar motion for any extended length of time. It's ok to have all three staves moving in similar motion for very short amounts of time, but try to avoid it as much as you can (unless that is the style from the beginning!)

9. QUESTION 3A – STYLE

Question 3a tests your ability to understand the harmonies and compositional techniques used by Romantic composers. In music, the Romantic era spans from the late 18th century right up to the mid 20th century. You'll need to be aware of the general characteristics of music at this period of time.

Here's a short list, in chronological order of birth year, of some of the composers who've been chosen by the ABRSM for question 3a over the last few years.

Cherubini (1760-1842)

Beethoven (1770-1827)

Schubert (1797-1828)

Mendelssohn (1809-1847)

Hofmann (1809-1894)

Verdi (1813-1901)

Brahms (1833-1897)

Saint-Saëns (1835-1921)

Grieg (1843-1907)

Stanford (1852-1924)

Bridge (1879-1941)

You might find that the composition was originally by someone much less well known though, for example

Weissenborn (1837-1888)

Somervell (1863-1937) or

Quilter (1877-1953)

The thing to remember though is that the composer will have written music in the **Romantic** style.

Over the past 10 years or so of ABRSM grade 7 papers, it seems that the chance of getting a piece by Mendelssohn is about one in five! So make sure you've listened to plenty of Mendelssohn pieces before you take the exam!

Generally speaking, Romantic music is an expression of human emotions: it tells a story. You can contrast it with Classical and Baroque music, which can sound a lot more mathematical, elegant or even simple in comparison to Romantic music.

Romantic music uses a lot of strong, dramatic contrasts, and it's normal for the music to explore a wide range of pitches, including large leaps or visits to both ends of the instrument's compass, as well as a wide range of dynamics - with both sudden and gradual changes.

In terms of harmony, Romantic music normally explores a wide range of keys and chords. Whereas in the classical era, a piece of music would tend to only modulate to a closely related key, and generally at a strategic point in the piece, in Romantic music these restraints are abandoned. You can expect a surprise modulation to almost any key, at any point in the music. In the same way, all kinds of chromatic alterations can appear, as well as dissonances, lovely rich harmonies with added 7ths and 9ths, augmented 6th chords and so on. But, Romantic era music is tonal - it's based on the major and minor system, so you won't find yourself having to write a piece based on a whole tone scale or anything as modern as that.

In terms of rhythm, Romantic music tends to use a wide range of rhythmic note values. You can contrast this with Baroque music, which often reused the same running quaver (or 8th note) figures for a really long time. Classical music tends to use phrases which are of an equal length - balance was a really important feature in the classical era. But in Romantic music, anything goes in terms of phrase length - they might be of unequal or equal lengths. In question 3a, suggested phrase lengths are marked out for you, but you don't have to stick to them exactly, if you don't want to.

In terms of melody, Romantic music is often built up using sequences or motifs, which are adapted and developed to create the rest of the piece. This is really important for you to understand, as you'll need to do the same! You need to look at the way the piece opens - does it move by step, leaps, or a combination? And then you should carry on in a similar way. Another thing to notice is the use of chromaticism - Romantic composers liked the added colour that using accidentals gives to a piece.

So, your composition will need to sound like it's from the Romantic era. The easiest and most enjoyable way to train your brain to recognise the Romantic style, Is to listen to plenty of Romantic music. Try to listen actively though, rather than passively. Listen for key changes, drama and tension, melodic leaps, big contrasts and notice how everything connects together. For even better results, listen while following a musical score. The best source for free scores of out-of-copyright music on the internet is at www.imslp.org - you'll find just about everything there, just a click or two away. If you put a little more work into it, and do something like work out the keys, chords and how certain effects have been achieved, you'll get an enormous benefit from the effort you put in.

To save you a bit of time, I've put together a Youtube playlist of music by Romantic era composers which has been composed or arranged for one instrument plus piano. The link is here: https://www.youtube.com/playlist?list=PLyZpSAfmPoZEqb7nKWMShyz7AzCtfofXi

I'm always adding to the playlist, so do let me know if you have video which would be a good addition to the list!

10. QUESTION 3A – PLAN OF ACTION

Here is a step-by-step plan for answering question 3a which is explained thoroughly in the next pages, and I'd recommend that you follow all the steps when you do your first few practice compositions. After a short while though, you'll probably want to adapt it to suit your own needs, and that's fine. Just make sure that you have looked at all the different aspects of the piece before you get started.

1. Take notice of the key, time, composer and instrument.

2. Sing through the given melody in your head

3. Analyse the harmony

4. Notice any similarities and differences

5. Analyse the melodic structure

6. Analyse the rhythmic structure

7. Look at how the parts combine with each other

8. Make a decision about aims for your composition

9. Compose!

11. QUESTION 3A – KEY, TIME, COMPOSER, INSTRUMENT

Hopefully it goes without saying that you need to look at the key signature and time signature before you start! But really, you need to look and think, not just look.

KEY

For the key, make sure you know whether the piece begins in the major or minor mode of the key signature. It might not be as obvious as you think - if you rely on looking for accidentals, for example, you can easily get mislead, and here are three reasons why:

a) In a minor key, all the notes from the melodic minor scale are available. In practice this means that in the key of A minor, for example, you can expect to find G naturals and F naturals, as well as G sharps and F sharps. If you go looking for a G# and find only a G natural, you can't assume it's C major.

b) The only notes which are given accidentals in a minor key are the 6th and 7th degrees of the scale. But it's quite common to find a piece which doesn't actually use these degrees of the scale at all, which means you won't be able to draw any conclusions that way.

c) At this level of exam, it's extremely likely that your composition will contain some elements of chromaticism - notes which are altered with accidentals because they sound nice, not because those accidentals are part of the minor key.

For example, this piece is in C major, but there's a G sharp at the start of bar 2. It's not there as part of A minor, it's actually a chromatic decoration.

Although accidentals can help in some situations, you need to look at the harmony to know for sure what the key is.

There are only two chords which can fix a key with any certainty in the ear of a listener, and those chords are I and V, the **tonic** and **dominant** chords.

So, you need to look at the melody in combination with the piano accompaniment and see which chords are being used. You will normally find that the first bar, and often the second bar as well, use chords I and V in the correct key.

TIME

At this grade, you should be completely confident about using any of the possible time signatures. Take a look at the time signature, and remind yourself what it actually means in terms of beats per bar, for example, 9/8 will be three beats per bar, or 6/4 will be two. This is important, because the way you write rhythms and the way you beam together fast notes always depends on the time signature.

COMPOSER

There's always a chance that it might be someone you've heard of, and whose music you know really well. Looking at the composer's name might help to jog your memory, to help you write in a similar style.

You might even know the piece itself - but don't try to write it out exactly as it was in the original!

INSTRUMENT

Finally, make sure you've noticed the solo instrument. You'll need to make sure that you don't write any notes which are not in the instrument's range of course, but also knowing what the music will sound like on that instrument will help you write idiomatically - which means "in a style fitting for the instrument".

Don't forget too, that if you're writing for a wind or brass instrument, you'll need to be careful about allowing the performer somewhere to breathe.

SING IT THROUGH

Step 2 is to sing it through. Try to hear each individual part in your head, and if possible, the parts combined with each other too.

Take a look at "How to Hear Music in Your Head" at the beginning of the course if you need help.

12. QUESTION 3A – HARMONIC STRUCTURE

You'll need to look at the harmony of the composition in two ways. Firstly, work out the chords by the letter name for example C major or G7.

Next, work out how those chords relate to each other by using Roman numerals. When you do this part, you'll also begin to see where the piece changes key, if at all. Pencil in all the information you can find as you go along - the more you know, the easier it should be to work out how to continue.

When you work out a chord by its letter name, you need to look for notes which make up a common triad, and ignore any passing notes or other types of melodic decoration.

Your melody needs to fit with the harmonic structure of the piece. This means that you need to:

- work out the implied chords for the entire piece
- write melody notes which fit each chord, according to the grammatical rules
- include non-chord notes, e.g. passing notes, auxiliary notes, suspensions and/or changing notes

Look at the first two beats of bar 5. The piano part makes a chord of C minor. The quaver (8th note) F is a passing note.

In the melody part you could use:

- C, Eb or G, as **chord notes**
- **Passing notes**, between any of the chord notes, e.g. C-D-Eb
- **Auxiliary notes**, to liven up any chord note e.g. C-B-C
- **Chromatic auxiliary notes**, again, to spice things up, e.g. G-F#-G (take care not to clash with the F natural though)

Suspensions are another useful type of melodic decoration, but you need to use them carefully. A suspension is most effective when it uses notes that are not already sounding in the piano part.

Bar 5 in the above example doesn't provide a good opportunity to use a suspension, but later in the same exercise there are some more appropriate places:

In bar 14 the piano part makes a dominant 7th chord in G minor, minus the 5th (i.e. D7 without an A). The melody part could complete the chord by having the A, and then the A could be suspended into bar 15, creating a dissonance with the bass note G.

The resolution can be held off until bar 16 in this case – making a nice long suspension to finish the end of the phrase.

Since the harmony changes to G major at this point (after previously being in G minor), delaying the B natural by avoiding adding the third in bar 15 also makes the key change more effective.

The following illustrates a possible way to write the suspension:

Try not to follow any dissonance with another dissonance - make sure any dissonance is resolved before writing another one (unless this is a feature elsewhere in the given material).

Watch out for clashes in the other parts, particularly if you use a chromatic note. Sometimes clashes will be appropriate, however.

In this opening, there is a "false relation" which means a semitone clash (F against F#) in bar 3. This is caused by the conflicting notes in the melodic G minor scale. It would be a good idea to use another false relation later on, if possible.

13. QUESTION 3A – SIMILARITIES & DIFFERENCES

Before you begin to compose, take a moment to quickly see whether any of the piano accompaniment contains repeated ideas, or whether the given section of the solo part is also used in the piano part at any point.

If you find that two bars or so are the same, think carefully about how you will deal with them. It's fine at this grade to actually repeat part of the composition note for note, if it fits what's going on in the piano part. At the lower grades I do discourage exact repetition, as the examiner wants to see your skills at creating something new, but in question 3a, noticing that something in the piano part has been repeated is quite important, and by reusing part of the solo melody you will show that you did actually notice.

Do look very carefully though, because sometimes two bars can be **almost** the same, with just one small difference which actually has a big effect. For example, a change of just one note by a semitone can launch the piece into a modulation.

If there is some repetition in the accompaniment, and it's copied from the given opening, you're in luck! You can copy some of the solo part without worrying about whether it will sound ok or not.

In this piece for example, bar 9 is a repetition of the material from bar 1 onwards, except it's an octave higher. We could, therefore, use the same melody notes as the oboe has in bar 1 onwards.

14. QUESTION 3A – MELODIC AND RHYTHMIC STRUCTURE

Check how the given opening is constructed. How much of it is conjunct (stepwise) and how much disjunct (leaping) motion?

Look at the shape of the phrase(s) and take notice of the actual intervals used in any disjunct motion (e.g. octave leaps) - make a note of anything that seems special or important.

What types of rhythm have been used? Which note values give the opening its character? Note down anything which seems to be characteristic, so that you can reuse those rhythms. It is important to be able to identify the elements of the given score which give the music its particular character, and to continue in the same way.

In the given opening below, we can describe the melody as conjunct to begin with, as it moves smoothly by step from Bb to D. It then falls by a 2nd to Bb, and the rest of the opening is built using only these two intervals – the 2nd and 3rd, plus the use of a repeated note.

Rhythmically the three beats of the bar are split 2:1, with the first 2/3 taken up by either a minim (half note), or repeated pitch. The last 1/3 of the bar is split into two notes – either straight quavers (8th notes) or the dotted quaver + semiquaver idea (dotted 8th + 16th).

These are the elements that we should then use to build out the rest of the composition – we are not limited to these ideas of course, but they should make up a large part of what comes next.

Look back at the chapters on Melodic Structure (5) and Rhythmic Structure (6) if you need some help with this.

132

15. QUESTION 3A – COMBINED PARTS

In question 3a, I recommend that you look at how the parts **combine** with each other to produce a whole piece, in terms of melody and rhythm.

You can gather information here which will help you make decisions in the rest of the piece - remember that you should always be looking for ways to create consistency, to give your piece a unified feel. If you have a couple of options of possible notes to write, for example, if you make your decision based on something that exists already in the piece, your decision will be justified.

Firstly, you might find that the solo part combines **melodically** with one of the piano staves at a certain interval. For example, it's common for a solo part to have the same rhythm as the right hand piano part but perhaps the melody is written a third higher or lower. It might even combine with the left hand instead, but this is less likely.

Secondly, take a look at the **harmony** which is produced by the combination of parts. Notice in particular which chord notes are doubled, and which are missed out. Look at the function of the solo part in terms of harmony - does it use notes which already exist in the piano part, or does it tend to complete the harmony by filling in a gap - such as a missing 3rd?

What sort of pitch distance is put between the solo and piano parts? You may find that the piano and solo parts intermingle around the same part of the stave, or in contrast, perhaps the piano part is much lower and the solo part pitched much higher, creating a larger distance. Also take a quick look for evidence of **imitation** - does the piano part imitate what the solo part just played, or vice-versa?

For example, from this given bar, you can see that the melody part follows the shape of the left hand piano part, but a (compound) third higher.

The melody part is higher than the piano part. And the melody part completes the triads in the harmony, supplying the missing G from the Gm second inversion chord, and the F# from the D major root position chord.

When you've collected some ideas, make a note of them on some scrap paper so that you can refer back to them quickly.

When you begin to compose, you'll be able to look back at your notes and make informed decisions about what to write. While a lot of the time you will probably be picking notes which help you conform to the **same** style as you've discovered, it's also of course possible to choose to do something **opposite** to what might be expected. Let's say the solo and piano tend to follow each other at an interval of a 3rd - at a certain point in the piece things may seem to be pointing towards a more dramatic section - perhaps the harmony is changing swiftly, the dynamics are getting louder and the rhythms faster - this would be a good place to break from the conformity of the piece briefly, and make your melody do something a bit more exciting.

The point is that the information you get from doing this exercise will help you to **decide** what to do - don't think of it as a set of rules that you need to discover and then follow blindly.

16. QUESTION 3A – MAKE A CHECKLIST

Now that you have taken a good, careful look at all aspects of the given opening and the accompaniment, make a concrete decision to base your composition on 3-4 specific stylistic features.

For example, you might to decide to include things like:

- triplet rhythms
- leaps of a 6th
- intervals of an augmented 2nd
- close harmony in 6ths with the r.h. piano

and so on.

The elements you choose should be the ones which you think really give the piece its **character**.

You should then aim to use those features in the rest of the piece - not necessarily in every bar, but as an overall plan for what you write.

When you finish your composition, go back to your checklist and make sure that you have enough of each stylistic feature within your part of the piece - if you don't, make a few alterations until you do.

17. QUESTION 3B – INTRODUCTION

There are three possible ways of writing an answer to question 3b, but you won't know until exam day what your options are, so it's a good idea to familiarise yourself with all the possible variations before the big day.

The three variations of this question are:

1. Composing from a harmonic progression with a **given** opening

2. Composing from a harmonic progression with your **own** opening

3. Composing **without** a given harmonic progression, but with a given opening

If you're given a harmonic progression, you'll also get an example opening. You have to use the chord progression exactly as it's given, but it's up to you whether you use the example opening or not. If you're not given a chord progression, then you will get an obligatory given opening which you have to continue from.

In all cases, you should write out the **complete** melody on the staves provided, including copying out the given opening if you are using it. Whichever type of question you are writing, there are some things which need to be done in every situation.

1. WRITE AN 8-BAR COMPOSITION

Your composition needs to be eight bars long in total (unless otherwise indicated). Don't forget that if there's an upbeat, the last bar will need to take that into account. Start numbering the bars from the first complete bar. The upbeat bar isn't numbered, and the last bar will be bar 8 in every case.

Your melody will also need to be well balanced. Usually this means two complimentary 4-bar phrases, ideally with a cadence at the end of the first, and definitely with a cadence at the end.

If your melody has an upbeat, you can make the second phrase start on an upbeat of the same value, at the end of bar 4.

2. INCLUDE FULL PERFORMANCE DIRECTIONS.

Unlike in question 3a, you **do** have to include performance directions for question 3b. If you did grades 5 and 6 you should be pretty used to this, but here's a quick recap of the essentials.

You must include a **tempo**, written above the first note, and an opening **dynamic** written below it. You then need to include other, musically meaningful dynamics **throughout** the piece. Make sure nothing is written in an ambiguous way, such as writing "ff" under a bar line instead of a note, and keep in mind any limitations of the instrument you are writing for - a flute will find it very hard to play its lowest notes at a fortississimo dynamic, for example.

You also need to include **articulation** - slurs where appropriate, and perhaps other stylistic articulations such as staccato or accents. Bowing direction symbols are **not** necessary.

Be consistent in the way you use articulations. If the given opening uses tenuto over a certain pattern of notes, make sure that when you write a similar pattern (melodic or rhythmic) elsewhere in the piece, you use tenuto there in the same way.

Also, don't forget to **copy over** the performance directions of the given opening as well as the notes, when you start your piece.

And of course, it goes without saying that you need to write your music out **carefully and neatly**. Use a pencil, and draw lines with a ruler if possible. If anything on the page is difficult to read, you might lose points, and you will definitely lose points for errors in your notation such as stems the wrong way round on notes, putting the wrong number of beats in a bar, or beaming notes in the wrong-sized groups, and so on.

18. QUESTION 3B – DEALING WITH A CHORD PROGRESSION

If you're given a chord progression, you'll be given a series of chords which fill up eight bars. The clef and key signature will be in place, as these will of course fix the pitch of the notes you're looking at, but normally there won't be a time signature in place.

Each chord will have three or four notes in it and will be written in any inversion. There won't be any rhythm given to these chords, but the notation used should give you an idea of how they are intended to be used in the composition. The way that the chords are written can look a bit off-putting at first glance, and you might be tempted to run a mile, but actually they are quite easy to understand.

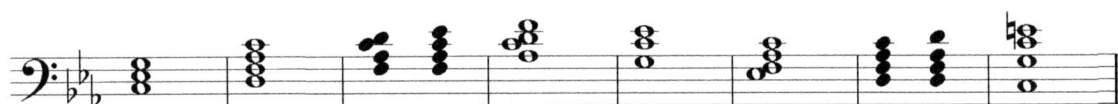

In this case for example, we're looking at a piece in the bass clef with three flats in the key signature. This means the first chord is C minor, and the harmony of C minor will last for the entire first bar. Bearing in mind the key signature of three flats, we can assume that the whole piece is going to be in C minor, since it's normal to start on the tonic, or perhaps dominant chord, but very unusual to begin on chord vi.

In the second bar we've got a four note chord. Four note chords will be a triad with an added note such as a 7th or 9th. You might need to re-stack the chord notes to figure out the base triad. In this case, we've got D diminished, which is D-F-Ab, with an added C on top, so this is chord ii°7 in root position. You'll need to go through and work out the Roman numeral name of each chord and pencil them in, so that you can see the harmonic structure more clearly.

In bar 3, the note heads are black to show you that the harmony lasts for less than a whole bar - you have two chords here, and how you divide up time between the chords will be up to you. For example, if you are writing in 4/4 for example, you could give each chord 2 beats worth, or you could choose to give the first chord three beats and the second chord one beat, and so on. It's up to you.

The name of the first of these two chords is less obvious to the eye, because it's not in root position. The notes are F, Ab, C and D. You need to restack these in thirds, to find out what the chord is. Restacked in thirds, the chord is D-F-Ab-C, so it's actually the same chord as the previous one, only this time because the bass note is F instead of D, it's in first inversion.

Take a moment now to work out the rest of the chords in this progression.

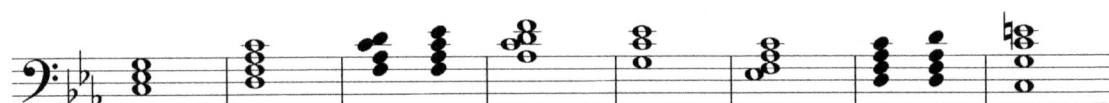

| Cm | D°7 | D°7 | Fm7 | D°7 | Cm | Fm7 | D°7 | D° | C |

The chord notes will tend to fall on the strongest beats of the bar. The strongest beat is the first beat, and subsequent beats will be weaker. Notes which are in between the main beats are off beats and the location where most of the melodic decoration will be found. There are exceptions though - you can use accented passing notes for example, as well as unaccented ones.

This is the basic way that chords become melody - by placing the chord notes themselves on stronger, more accented positions within the bar than non-chord notes, the harmony can become evident.

You can use any type of non-chord note you want (passing notes, auxiliary notes, suspensions, anticipations and changing notes), which means you do have a lot of options as you place each note down.

Here are two things you'll want to watch out for:

Firstly, don't move from a chord note to another one via a non-chord note which isn't one of the **standard** decorations mentioned above (passing notes etc.). Avoid non-chord notes which you can't categorise – they will cause your melody to move in unusual ways and will risk making it sound awkward.

Secondly, when you have one chord to use for a whole bar, pay attention to which notes are falling on and off the beat. It's a common error to focus only on the first beat of the bar and to let the rest of it flow as it will, without keeping the harmony under close control. In 4/4 for example, you would normally expect a chord note on each of the four crotchet (quarter note) beats, or at least on the two minim (half note) positions. If you place a non-chord on beat 3 (which is relatively strong), you risk altering the implied harmony at that point.

Here for example, because beat three has the note A, the brain/ear will process the harmony here as A minor. If the intended chord is C major, this will be a problem.

On the other hand, the C on the third beat here, which falls to G on the 4th beat, ensures that the correct harmony of C major is implied.

Although the chord progression contains chords given in various different inversions, you don't need to try to map this out in your composition in any way. The lowest note at any point of a chord can be any note of the chord you prefer. So for example, although a C minor chord might be notated in 2nd inversion, it doesn't mean you have to use a G as the lowest note - you can use C, Eb or G.

19. QUESTION 3B – MAKE YOUR OWN CHORD PROGRESSION

If the question in your exam paper doesn't contain a chord progression, it doesn't mean that chords and harmony will not be assessed - quite the opposite in fact. If there is no given chord progression, you will need to figure one out for yourself. I would strongly recommend not leaving it up to chance, or where the music seems to take you. Your harmonic structure needs to be logical and convincing, and you will get better results if you take a moment to plan out what you are going to do.

You'll need to start by working out the key of the given opening of course. At this stage you should have no difficulty in working out the key based on the key signature and melody notes used in the first bar. Using Roman numerals, note down the chords that have been used so far - you'll normally get around 2 bars to start you off.

Next sketch out a framework for your eight bars. You're going to balance the composition into two four-bar phrases, so mark that out.

At the end of the first phrase, you need to work out some kind of cadence. You have some options here, but two possibilities which are guaranteed to work are:

1) use an imperfect cadence, so you'll land on chord V on the first beat of bar 4 or,

2) modulate to a related key and use V-I or V7-I, with I in the new key landing on the first beat of bar 4.

The easiest keys to modulate to are the ones which are most closely related, which are the relative major or minor key, the dominant, or the subdominant.

If you are stuck for ideas, a very typical modulation pattern is to use a major chord II (perhaps with an added 7th), followed by chord V, which will actually be the tonic chord in the new key.

For example if you start out in G minor, you can easily modulate to D major, using A major or A7. You could do exactly the same from G major too.

At the end of your piece, you should end up in the original key, with a perfect cadence. The tonic chord of a perfect cadence should land on a stronger beat than the dominant chord.

After sketching in the given opening and two cadences, there won't be a huge number of chords to add in to complete your harmonic plan. You should change the harmony either once or twice a bar on average, so you only have about 3 bars left to be creative with.

While I think it's a good idea to plan out the harmony of the first four-bar phrase, you might want to leave the second phrase unplanned - it's up to you. If you are quite confident about writing a convincing melody based on sequences and so on, then phrase 2 will write itself to a certain extent, as you'll base it closely on phrase 1. If you're less certain about doing that well, then I'd suggest you plan out chords for bars 5-7 as well, in order to make sure that your composition changes chord often enough, and uses a wide enough variety of chords.

The chords you choose are up to you, but here are some tips.

- While it's possible to write a harmonic progression which only uses primary chords (I, IV or V) it won't sound very interesting.

- It's not possible to write a harmonic progression which only uses secondary chords (ii, iii, vi and vii) without destroying the tonality of the piece. For example if your piece is in C major and you write only chords E minor, D minor and A minor, you will have changed the key centre of the entire piece to modal form of A minor. The **tonic** and **dominant** chords are essential for fixing the key.

- Chord vii° sounds a lot like V7 and is best treated as the same chord.

- Chord V is usually used in the major form, even in a minor key.

- Augmented chords are best avoided.

- Chords with added 7ths or even 9ths will add colour and interest. At the very least, aim to use V7 leading to the tonic.

- The supertonic 7th is also quite easy to use and flows nicely to chord V. II7 works as a major, minor or diminished chord, so it's really flexible. E.g. in C major, try D-F-A-C (ii7), D-F#-A-C (II7) or D-F-Ab-C (ii°7).

- If you are very confident, you can even consider using altered chords such as the beautifully juicy Neapolitan 6th, or one of the augmented 6th chords - the Italian, French or German. These chords are explained in the section 4, lesson 5.

20. QUESTION 3B – MAKING A MELODY WITH FORM

The biggest mistake I see in students' compositions, is that they often seem to be like a rambling walk in the countryside, with no path planned and no destination in mind.

Harmony works with melody to help fix some signposts within a composition, for example, cadences are great at signalling the end of a phrase. Your brain is so used to hearing the typical cadences in Western music, that it will fill in the gaps for you and whether you realise it or not, you are predicting what comes next. Your brain expects a tonic chord after a dominant chord at the end of a piece, and if it doesn't happen, you end up feeling surprised or even confused.

Musical **form** works in a similar way, in that it helps to add signposts that will prevent your melody from sounding random and directionless.

DESCRIBING FORM IN MUSIC

We'll use capital letters to mark out musical form. The first idea in the piece will be called A. A new idea will be called B and so on. You can change a musical idea in subtle ways without changing it completely.

Here's a simple tune by John Alcock [1715-1806].

Phrase A runs for the first two bars. It's characterised as a quaver or eighth note passage in mostly conjunct (stepwise) motion.

Phrase B runs for the next two bars and although the rhythm is the same apart from at the very end, the melody is now mostly created with disjunct motion (leaps of a third or more), so it's clearly different in character.

Bars 5-6 are a repeat of the beginning, so we'll call this A again.

The last two bars start the same way as phrase B, but this is the end of the section and we move towards a cadence with some ornaments and longer note values. You could call this B1, a slightly altered B.

Here's the same beginning, but continued without any thought about form. Play it through. How does it sound to you?

It feels like it's just running around random notes, killing time until it gets to the tonic Bb at the end. You can't make any predictions as you listen, because there's nothing to latch on to. Your brain needs a certain amount of repetition - whether of rhythm, melody, harmony or all three, so that it can make those predictions and ultimately make sense of the music. If I was going to describe the form of this piece, I'd only really able to say it is A-B: two bars of A, followed by a very long and wandering B.

So, you need form. What sort of form should you aim for?

A-B-A1-B1 is a good plan, because it's balanced evenly and has some repetition.

A-A1-B-A is good as well - the last phrase A will not be identical to the beginning, since it will include a cadence and suitable ending, of course.

What you want to avoid is A-B-C-D, which will be something different every two bars,

You also want to be careful not to repeat too much note-for-note as well – A – A – A – A!

This is where **sequences** come in handy - you can repeat phrase A more or less exactly, but starting on a **scale step higher** for example, and you'll have made another A, but this time slightly altered.

142

21. QUESTION 3B – ACCIDENTALS & CHROMATICS

Accidentals can be either diatonic or chromatic, and they can appear in your composition for any of three separate reasons.

1) They might be necessary as part of the minor key. Melodies use the notes from the melodic minor scale (i.e. both the raised and unraised 6th and 7th degrees of the scale), so you could expect to find G# and F# in the key of A minor, for example. These are **diatonic** accidentals.

2) They might occur because of modulation. If the music is changing key, accidentals will need to be added for the new key. These kind of accidentals are also **diatonic**, because they belong to the new key that you're modulating to.

3) They might occur just as decorative notes, for example as auxiliary or passing notes. When they are used just for decoration, accidentals are **chromatic**, which means they are they to add colour, and they are not notes which normally exist in that key.

USING ACCIDENTALS IN MINOR KEYS

When you plan out the harmonic structure of your piece, you will definitely need to be using a good number of **dominant** chords. Dominant chords have a strong pull towards the tonic, which is brought about by the semitone movement of the leading note to the tonic note. This means that in a minor key, you need to make sure the leading note has been raised up by a semitone, using an accidental, whenever chord V is the harmony implied underneath. Don't forget also that chord vii° usually works the same way as chord V, so vii° will also need a raised leading note if it leads to the tonic.

However, sometimes you will probably choose **not** to raise the leading note. You can use all the notes which are available in the melodic minor scale, so in the key of A minor you can use G naturals and F naturals, as well as the raised versions of those notes. Using a G natural gives you the opportunity to use chord VII, the major chord formed on the unraised 7th degree of the scale. This is a really useful chord, as it's the dominant chord of the relative major key (C major), which is chord III. Within a minor key then, you can use VII and III as major chords, combined with each other, to good effect.

You will also want to think about using accidentals to avoid **awkward intervals** in a minor key. The F# from the A minor melodic scale can be used to iron out the augmented 2nd between F and G#, for example. Augmented intervals are not illegal, and in some situations they can be used to produce a nice effect - as always, you need to be consistent in what you do. If the opening of the composition obviously avoids augmented 2nds then that's how you should continue, but if they are used as a feature of the opening, you'll want to use more of them elsewhere.

With all added accidentals, be especially vigilant about using them on the beat. As you know, notes which land squarely on the beat usually need to be part of the harmony. If you are using chord V, you need a raised leading note. But on the other hand, if you are using chord VI in a minor key piece, you want to make sure that the submediant note hasn't been raised up. For example in A minor, chord VI is F major, so you'd need to make sure that any F sounding at that point was F natural and not F# from the melodic minor scale.

ACCIDENTALS IN MODULATION

The most common way to modulate is through the use of a **pivot chord**, which is a chord that exists in the old and new keys, followed **immediately** by chord V(7) - I in the new key. You'll need to add accidentals which are relevant for the new key.

ACCIDENTALS AS CHROMATICS

Auxiliary notes are the most common way to introduce chromatics which are just decorative. The chromatic auxiliary note slips between two identical pitches, and of course you can also split a single note up to achieve this affect too.

Adding a lower chromatic auxiliary note gives a major feel to the melody. Adding an upper chromatic auxiliary note gives a darker, more minor feel to the melody.

Whether you choose an upper or lower auxiliary will also probably depend on the general direction of your melody: what's coming next. If the melody rises, a lower auxiliary note usually works well, whereas is the melody is falling the opposite is true.

Chromatic passing notes can also be used. They can make the step between two notes more interesting. A good spot is when the mediant rises to the dominant, for example E, F, G in C major. You can raise the F to F# for a quick visit to G major, even if it only last for a beat or so.

Chromatic passing notes can also be used between two notes that are a tone or whole step apart, such as slotting a C# between C and D. Use sharps when the melody rises, and flats when it falls.

As always, the trick to a good composition is to be **consistent** but not overly **repetitive**. If you choose to use chromatic decoration in your piece, then it should happen at various points all the way through, and not, for example, only in the first half. If you do only want to use a very minimal amount of chromatics, then use them in a logical place, such as the bars where your melody is going to climax, and combine the chromatics with other signals such as an increase in dynamics or generally higher pitches used.

COMPOSITION EXERCISES

1. Compose an 8-bar melody using the following chord progression. You may use the given opening if you want to. Choose from trombone or cello and state your chosen instrument. Include performance directions.

2. Compose a melody of at least 8 bars using the given opening, for clarinet (at concert pitch) or violin. State which instrument you have chosen and include relevant performance directions.

3. Compose a melody to fit with the given accompaniment. Write the melody for violin. Suggested phrase marks are indicated.

COMPOSITION MODEL ANSWERS

The following are example answers – many answers are possible of course! For reference, chords have been added to the chord progression question – but you do not need to add the chord names on to the stave when you submit your answer paper in the exam.

1. (Key: G minor, Instrument: cello)

2. (Key: E minor, Instrument: violin)

3. Key F minor

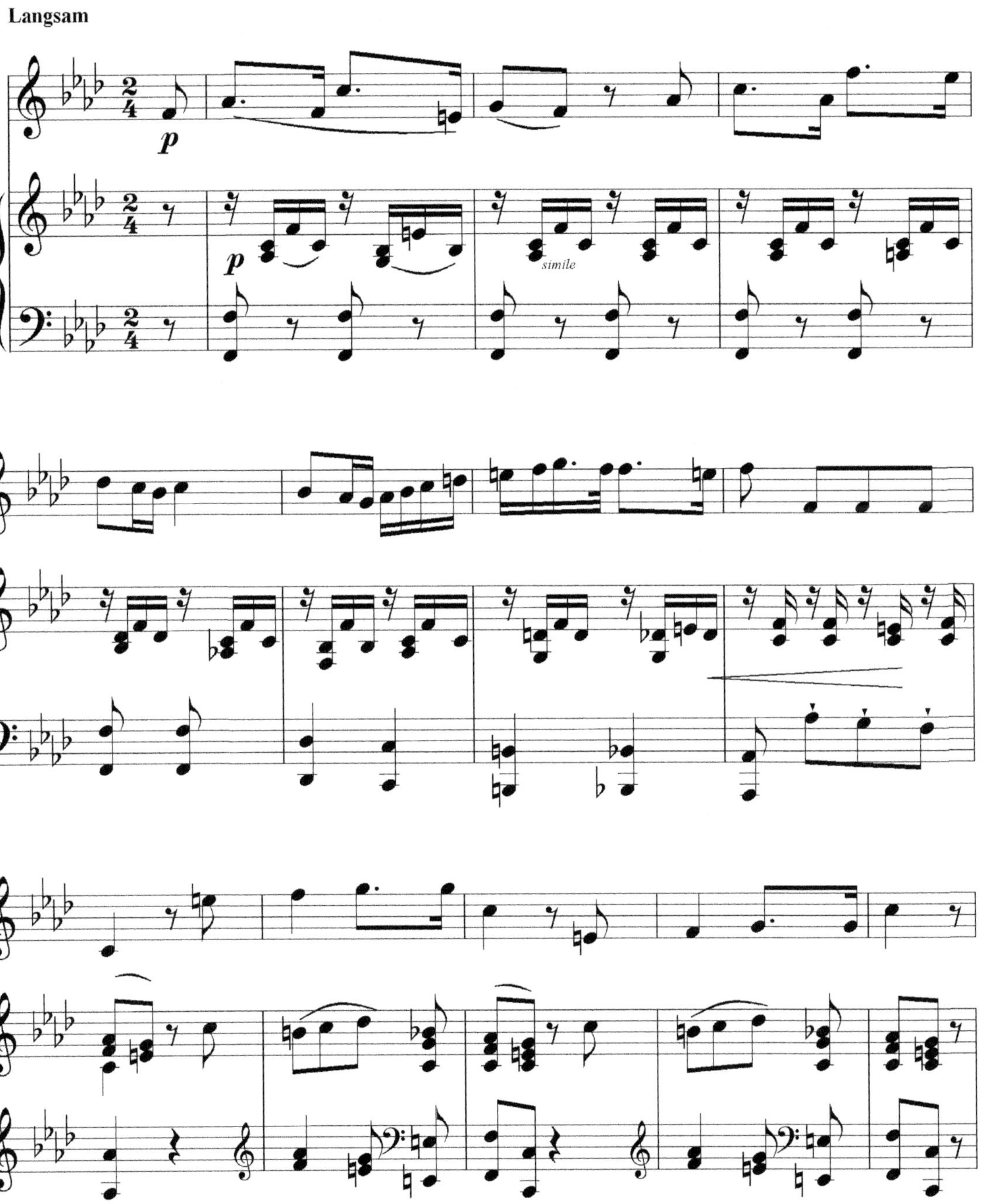

SECTION 4 - SCORE READING

1. HOW TO EXCEL AT SCORE READING

The type of questions that come up in the grade 7 ABRSM score reading sections are ones you can normally prepare well for. Certain topics nearly always come up (e.g. transposing horn parts), so the best way to ensure that you are fully prepared for the exam is to do **as much practice as possible**.

Apart from this course, you can practise in the following ways:

- Active listening with a score
- Use the ABRSM grade 7 Workbook
- Use the ABRSM past exam papers and model answers

ACTIVE LISTENING WITH A SCORE

The absolute best method to getting good at finding your way around a score and learning about all the terms and symbols found within them, is to **look at lots of them!**

The amazing website www.imslp.org contains an enormous database of copyright-free "classical" music scores and audio recordings which you can use free of charge (you can donate too though).

Try this method on a regular basis (two to three times a week is a good plan).

1. Choose an era to focus on: Baroque, Classical, Romantic or Modern.
2. Go to https://en.wikipedia.org/wiki/List_of_classical_music_composers_by_era and select a composer – it could be a famous one, or obscure – it's up to you.
3. Go to www.imslp.org and search for the composer's name, and pick a random score to open.
4. Either use the available audio on imslp.org, or visit www.youtube.com and search for a recording of the piece you chose. Some Youtube videos even show moving scores – try putting "score" in the search terms to find these.
5. **Listen** to the music while you follow the score. Make notes about:
    - The instruments used
    - The texture (thick or sparse...)
    - The harmony (traditional, exotic...)
    - The performance directions (few or many...)
    - How the composer achieves certain effects (drama, mood change...)
    - What your overall impression of the piece is
    - Similarities and differences as the music progresses
6. **Write** down any terms or symbols that are in the score, which are unfamiliar to you. Look them up and learn them.
7. Choose three or four bars that you like the sound of, or that are particularly interesting, and **copy** them out. Either do it by hand, or with a music notation software (www.musescore.org is free and excellent). You will discover quite a lot about the music by doing this, which you didn't notice just by looking at it! Play through the individual parts, and combinations of parts.
8. See if you can work out the key and harmony of the extract you copied. Test yourself on some intervals between instruments. Try to describe in words what the music sounds like. Transpose parts into concert pitch where possible.
9. Research the piece on the internet. Try searching for "programme notes" plus the name of the piece, for more in depth descriptions and a historical/analytical perspective.

ABRSM Resources

The "Grade 7 Workbook" published by the ABRSM contains lots of practice questions. Each year the ABRSM publishes past papers of the previous years' exams. It's essential to work through a good selection of these, so that you know what to expect on the day. Model answers are available as separate booklets.

All ABRSM publications can be purchased directly from their shop which can be found at www.shop.abrsm.org. Alternatively, you can also find their resources (including second hand copies) on Amazon. It's always worth checking Ebay too, as many people get rid of their resources once they have taken the exam!

2. NAVIGATING A SCORE

At Grade 7, it is expected that you can find your way around any kind of musical score – which means that you know which instruments are playing, which families and sections they belong to, and how many players are required.

ORDER OF INSTRUMENTS

The **order** of instruments in a score from top to bottom is normally the same. Knowing where each instrument "lives" within the score will help you to find your way around much quicker.

In the woodwind family, the flute section comprises the flute and sometimes piccolo, the clarinet section comprises clarinet and sometimes bass clarinet, and so on. The **standard** orchestral instruments are marked in **bold**.

The order of families and sections is this:

1. Woodwind

1.	Piccolo		5.	**Clarinet**
2.	**Flute**		6.	Bass clarinet
3.	**Oboe**		7.	**Bassoon**
4.	Cor Anglais		8.	Contrabassoon

2. Brass

1.	**French horn**		3.	**Trombone**
2.	**Trumpet**		4.	**Tuba**

3. Percussion

4. Harp

5. Piano

6. Strings

1.	**Violin**		3.	**Cello**
2.	**Viola**		4.	**Double bass**

Instrument Names in Other Languages

You need to be able to identify all the **names** of the standard orchestral instruments in English, Italian, French and German. For the most part, they tend to be quite similar, for example in German you can find a "Klarinette", or in Italian a "clarinetto".

Some of the more confusing translations are:

- "Tromba" = trumpet (Italian)
- "Trombe" = trumpets (Italian)
- "Alto" = viola (French)

Some of the less common translations which do occasionally get tested in the Grade 7 exam are:

- "Piatti" = cymbals (Italian)
- "Gran cassa" = bass drum (Italian)
- "Faggotto" = bassoon (Italian)
- "Pauken"= timpani/kettle drums (German)

Required Number of Players: Wind and Brass

In the left margin of the page, the score will usually tell you exactly **how many** players are required for each woodwind and brass section.

In the example score here, three flutes are required. The top stave accommodates flutes 1 and 2, and a second stave is needed for flute 3. Flute 1 plays the higher notes, and flute 2 the lower notes. The flute section is joined with a thin bracket.

The cor Anglais is a single player, so no number is written.

The woodwind family is outlined with a thicker bracket.

Four horns are required, two parts are written on each stave. No other brass instruments are required in this particular score, so a thick bracket outlines the horns AND brass section.

REQUIRED NUMBER OF PLAYERS: STRINGS

In the string family, a large number of violins, violas and cellos are used in a standard symphony orchestra. Numbers will vary, but you could expect around 20 violins, 10 violas and 10 cellos. Doubles basses are usually fewer – perhaps 5 or 6.

Because so many violins are used, they are normally divided into two sections, named "violin 1" and "violin 2". Unlike with the wind and brass instruments, this number does NOT refer to the exact number of individual players, but to about half of the entire section (i.e. around ten violins). Violins 1 and 2 are normally written on separate staves. Each "half" section is sometimes then divided again, so that two parts may appear on one stave, dividing the section into four separate parts (for example).

The violas normally reside on one stave and may be split into two or even three parts. The same goes for the cellos and double basses.

When one string instrument also has an important solo part, such as a violin in a violin concerto, there will be one extra stave set aside for the solo instrument, and the others string staves will be written as normal.

In a string quartet, the four instruments used are two violins ("first" and "second"), viola and cello. There is no double bass part.

INSTRUCTIONS FOR SPLITTING/COMBINING SECTIONS

One stave can hold music for two or more separate parts. When only one part is written on a stave, the normal stem direction is used ("stems up" for notes below the middle line, and vice versa).

When two parts are written on one stave, they are usually identified by the direction of the stems – one part will be all "stems up" and the other "stems down":

The term "**divisi a**" means "split into", and is usually abbreviated to "**div.**". Here the violas are instructed to split into 3 groups. One group will play the top note of the chords, the second group will play the middle notes, and the third group will play the low notes.

Notice that the stem directions are not dependent on the parts here.

The terms "**a2**" (Italian/French) and "**zu 2**" mean "both players". This term is used when two players share a stave (for instance, two flutes), but only one part is written on the stave. The instruction shows that both players should play the same part. The term "a 3", for example would mean "all three players".

When the composer only wants **one** player to play, but two of them share a stave, the term "**solo**" is used. The term "**unisono**", or "**unis.**" for short, means "all together", and shows that all players in the section should play. The term "**tutti**" means the same.

155

MEASURED OR REPEATED NOTE VALUES

In order to save money on ink, and to declutter a score, it is quite common to find repeated short note values such as quavers, semiquavers or demisemiquavers (eighth, sixteenth or thirty-second notes) written in an **abbreviated** form.

Instead of writing the fast note values in the standard way, a single beam is used, with slashes through the stems of the notes. The repeated note is only written once. The number of slashes will indicate the note value required. In the following example, there are two lines on each note (a beam and a slash), so the required note value is a semiquaver (sixteenth note).

Written in full, the same passage will look like this:

Don't confuse this symbol with a "tremolando", which is a string technique and uses the same symbol. The difference is that with measured note values, the term "trem." Is NOT used. If you are asked to explain this symbol in words, write "repeated, measured [semiquavers]".

ALTERNATIVE PASSAGES

The term "**ossia**" means "or" and is used when an **alternative** passage is available, which could be easier, or more difficult, to play. The ossia passage may (for example) be an octave lower, or use a less complicated rhythm. Sometimes it is used when the original manuscript may have existed with different versions at different times. The ossia passage is written in smaller sized notes, and often uses dotted bar lines to show where it fits.

This ossia from Spohr's 4th Clarinet Concerto shows an alternative passage with a different pitch and rhythm.

3. COMPOSITIONAL TECHNIQUES

In the grade 7 music theory exam, questions on compositional techniques can range from describing similarities and differences, to explaining or locating specific techniques within the score.

SIMILARITIES AND DIFFERENCES

You may be asked to compare two sections of the score and comment on the **similarities** and **differences**. This is a kind of "spot the difference" question. It's important to be as precise as possible in your answer, and avoid vague generalisations.

Changes/similarities to look out for:

- Pitch
- Rhythm
- Dynamics
- Articulation (e.g. accents, slurs, staccato etc.)
- Key
- Tempo
- Instrumentation (which instruments are playing)
- Expression (e.g. using Italian terms or symbols)

HOW DOES THE COMPOSER ACHIEVE AN EFFECT?

Typical questions ask **how the composer achieves** a feeling of strength, climax, drama or change of mood. You'll need to examine the same aspects of the music as listed above, but look in particular for things which fit the question.

- A sense of heightened drama or climax is normally achieved by making the music **faster**, **higher**, **louder**, or a combination of these.
- A feeling of strength could be achieved by **using more instruments** (especially powerful ones like French horns), and/or increased **dynamics** particularly in the lower register.
- A change of mood is often brought about by changing any of the items listed above, and usually several will be changed for a clear contrast.

PHRASES

You might be asked to mark out the **phrase structure** of the piece with brackets, or to say whether the piece consists of "regular phrases", but what is a phrase and how do you identify one?

A phrase is to music what a sentence or clause is to writing. In writing, you need to use sentences if you want to make sense.

At the end of a sentence, you use a full stop (period), to signify that the sentence has finished. In music, the same is most often achieved with a **perfect cadence** (V-I).

In writing, a sentence is often broken up into shorter sections called "clauses". The end of a clause is signified by a comma. The comma tells the reader that that particular part of the sentence is finished, but that there will be another part to follow. In music, this is achieved by an **imperfect cadence** (any chord followed by V), or **interrupted cadence** (V-VI).

Phrases are often used in pairs, with a "questioning" phrase (imperfect cadence) followed by an "answering" phrase (perfect cadence).

Things to look out for:

- Cadences are sometimes achieved with slightly **longer note values**, compared to the rest of the phrase. Looking at the note values used can help you locate the end of each phrase.
- Phrases can be split up by **rests** – so rests are another clue, and easy to spot quickly.
- **Dynamics** normally align with the start (and sometimes end) of a phrase.
- **Repetitions** can help you work out the phrase structure. For example, an "answering phrase" might use similar rhythm, but with different melody notes.
- Patterns in the **beaming** may provide a clue to where a phrase starts. For example, where a phrase begins on an upbeat, it's common for this note not to be beamed back to the notes in the previous phrase.

In this example ("Davidsbündlertanz" by Schumann), there are two four-bar phrases. Box A shows the imperfect cadence (i-V) at the end of phrase one (B minor), and box B shows the perfect cadence (V7-I) at the end of phrase two (modulation to D major).

In box C, notice that the quaver (eighth note) B is not beamed back to the previous notes – this is a good clue that it's the starting note of a new phrase. If you look at the rhythms, you will see that phrase two is almost exactly the same as phrase one. Can you find the difference in the rhythm?

Motifs

A **motif** is an easily recognisable, short musical idea, which is used as a seed to grow new music from. Repeated use of a motif throughout a composition helps to glue it together as a unified piece of music. Motifs are most often defined by their rhythm. The most famous motif in classical music is probably the first four notes of Beethoven's 5th Symphony:

Melodic Sequences

A **melodic sequence** is section of music which is repeated at a different pitch. In this simple sequence, notes 1-5 are repeated but each is a scale-step higher. This is an example of a **rising sequence**, as the repetition is higher pitched. You can also find **descending sequences**.

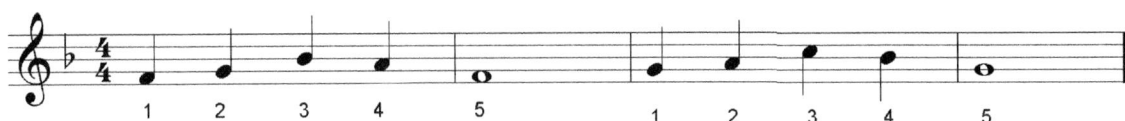

Like the motif, the sequence is used as a unifying technique – to ensure that a composition is built on connected ideas. The difference is that a motif tends to retain its rhythmic character and is normally quite short, whereas a sequence preserves its melodic character and can be considerably longer.

A sequence which introduces some minor changes which do not impact the overall character of the melody are described as **not exact**. Here, the sequence has a minor change on the second beat:

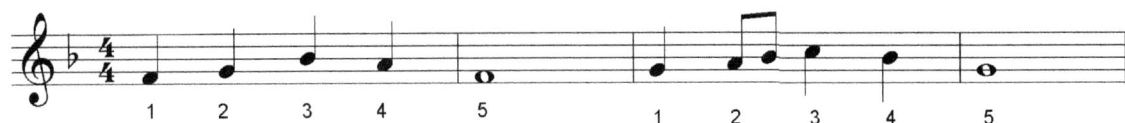

IMITATION

Imitation happens when a section of music is **repeated** in a different part, or instrument, or pitch, straight away like a kind of **echo**. In keyboard music, imitation could occur between the right and left hand staves, or even on a single stave which has been divided into a higher and lower part.

Here is an example of imitation from Saint-Saëns Clarinet Sonata (1st movement).

The piano plays C-Bb-Ab, which is immediately echoed in the clarinet part at the same pitch (transpose down a major 2nd into concert pitch!)

Imitation can be **melodic**, which means the entire melody is copied (as above), or just **rhythmic**. In rhythmic imitation, the rhythm is copied but the melody notes are changed. Here, the flute and clarinet use the same rhythm, but the echo moves in a different melodic direction, and by a different interval:

PARTS CROSS

The phrase "**parts cross**" means that between two parts, the higher one moves downward in pitch so far, that it becomes the lower one.

For example, in this passage for two clarinets, clarinet 1 begins on a higher pitched note than clarinet 2. But by the end of the phrase, the clarinet 1 is playing at a lower pitch than the second clarinet (see the boxed area).

Pedal

A **pedal** is a repeated note, (usually the **tonic** or **dominant** in the prevailing key) which is either **repeated** or **sustained** (held for some time), while the harmony **changes** above it. It gets its name from the foot pedal on the organ, which can sustain a note easily while the players' hands change

the harmony. Most often, the pedal occurs in the bass line of a piece.

Here, there is a tonic pedal on C in the bass, while the harmony changes above (Am, G, F, Dm, C):

A pedal can also occur **above** the bass, in which case it is an **inverted pedal**. A pedal which happens in a middle part can also be called an **inner pedal**. A pedal which uses **both** the tonic and dominant notes is a **double pedal**.

This pedal on B (dominant) is an inverted, (or inner), pedal, which is **sustained** (held). The chords are i, V7, i, ii°, V.

To find a pedal **quickly**, scan the score for a note which is repeated several times, or look out for long note values which fill the whole bar or more. Next, check that the harmony is actually **changing** at the same time. A long held bass note on its own is not a **pedal**, unless the harmony changes too.

4. INTERVALS AND PITCH

In the Grade 7 music theory exam, questions relating to intervals and pitch normally involve some **other** aspect of music theory which makes them a bit more complicated.

Most often, you'll have to transpose at least one note into concert pitch in order to find the solution. At other times, you might need to deal with a less familiar clef, and of course, you need to know all the relevant terminology of intervals, as well as how to work out intervals themselves.

At this stage, you should already know how intervals work, and that a "melodic" interval is formed between two consecutive notes and a "harmonic" interval is formed between two simultaneous notes. If you have any doubts about naming intervals (as "diminished", "augmented", "compound" and so on, look back at Grade 5 theory!)

TRANSPOSING TO CONCERT PITCH

In order to work out an interval, all notes must be converted to **concert pitch** before you do anything else. Get some scrap manuscript paper to work your answer out on, as it's difficult to keep all the information in your head!

The following instruments are already written at concert pitch (in other words, they are not transposing instruments):

- Flute, oboe, bassoon, trombone, tuba, violin, viola, cello, harp, piano, harpsichord

The following instruments transpose **at the octave**, meaning that the written note is an octave higher or lower than concert pitch:

- Piccolo (transpose up into concert pitch)
- Double bass (transpose down into concert pitch)

The following are transposing instruments in different keys:

- Clarinet and trumpet in Bb (or "si b" (Italian/French) or "B" (German)) (transpose down a major 2nd)
- Clarinet in A (or "la") (transpose down a minor 3rd)
- Clarinet in Eb (or "mi b") (transpose up a minor 3rd)
- Bass clarinet in Bb (transpose down an octave and a major 2nd)
- Bass clarinet in A (transpose down an octave and a minor 3rd) (rare)
- Cor Anglais and French horn in F (or "fa") (transpose down a perfect 5th)

Clarinets, trumpets and horns can be found in several transposition keys, so the transposition key (e.g. "cl. in Bb") is always given.

Bass clarinets and cors Anglais are always in the same transposition key, so it is not given and you will need to remember that they transpose! (Bass clarinets in A are always marked as such).

Remember that when a C clef is used, the centre of the clef surrounds the line where **middle C** (not any old C!) is found:

How to Work out an Interval

To work out any interval, first work out what both notes are at **concert pitch**, then write them using the **same clef**, so that the interval can be calculated more easily. Always count an interval from the **lower sounding note**, (regardless of how they are written in the original score).

Here's a harmonic interval between cor Anglais and cello. First take the cor Anglais note, and transpose it into concert pitch by putting it down a perfect 5th (B) (using the treble clef).

Next, take the cello note, and put that into the same clef as the first note. This is D just above middle C, so it's the D at the bottom of the stave.

Finally, work out the interval between D-B – it's a major 6th.

Other Terms for Intervals

1. A **chromatic semitone** is the same thing as an **augmented unison**. It occurs when the same letter name is used for both notes, but one is raised or lowered by a semitone with an accidental.

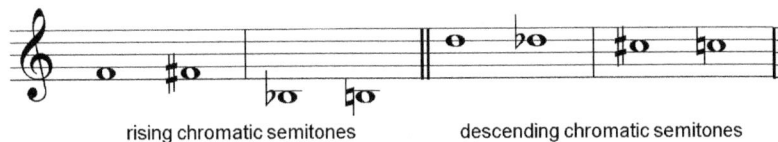

rising chromatic semitones   descending chromatic semitones

2. A **unison** occurs when both (or all) notes are exactly the same **sounding** pitch. These three instruments are sounding in unison – all of them are playing D below middle C (don't forget that the double bass sounds an octave lower than written!)

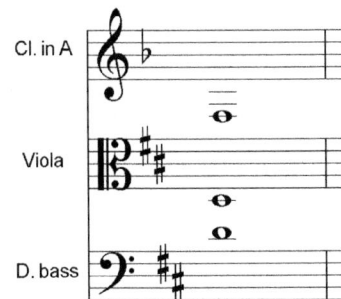

3. An **enharmonic equivalent** is the same pitch spelled a different way, for example C# and Db. Here are some examples:

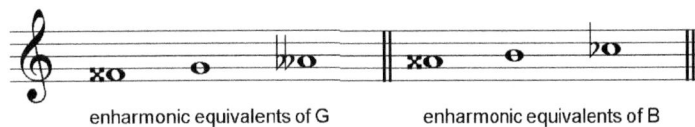

enharmonic equivalents of G   enharmonic equivalents of B

4. The term "**8va.......**" (or "8ve") is written above the stave, to show that the written notes should be played an octave higher. This term is used in order to avoid excessive ledger lines, which can be awkward to read and messy on the page. The line will show how far the octave displacement needs to be continued. After an "8va..." sign, you will normally find the term "**loco**", which means "in place" – or at the normal pitch.

5. HARMONY

Before you begin studying for the Grade 7 music theory exam, you should already know:

- how to identify the basic triads/chords found in diatonic keys – major, minor and diminished
- how to use the extended Roman numeral system to name chords and their positions (e.g. IVa, ivc etc.)
- how to identify key, including change of key

In order to correctly identify chords at Grade 7, you need to start by making sure you know the precise **sounding** pitches of each note in the chord – so read the chapter on "Intervals and Pitch" before beginning this chapter.

In this chapter we will look at:

- Added 7th chords including the major supertonic 7th (or "secondary dominant")
- Added 9th chords

- Key and the dominant 7th chord
- The Neapolitan 6th chord
- Diminished 7th chords
- Augmented 6th chords

ADDED 7TH CHORDS INCLUDING THE MAJOR SUPERTONIC 7TH

Any triad can become an "added 7th" chord, by adding the note a 7th above the root. The most common added 7th chords are V7 and ii7, but any chord can have a 7th added for extra colour.

Most often, the added 7th chord leads to the chord which is a **perfect 5th lower**. For example, V7 normally leads to I, and ii7 normally leads to V.

You are likely to also come across a chromatically altered chord ii7, changed into a **major** II7 – this is known as a "secondary dominant" chord. For example, in C major, chord ii is D minor. However, the dominant chord of G major is D major, so the chord might be altered to D-F#-A-C (II7) leading to the dominant G major chord.

When II7 is used, it does not necessarily mean the music has modulated. Although it can be used in a true modulation, it is also sometimes used simply for added interest. You will need to check what comes next, in order to know whether a modulation has taken place.

For example, a chord progression like this: C-D7-G-C-F-C-G will not have modulated to G major – the music does not remain in the new key long enough, and an F major chord doesn't occur in the key of G major. Compare C-D7-G-D-G-C-Am-D – the tonic C is not returned to immediately after the first G chord; instead the repeated D major chord reinforces the change of key. The last three chords would be I-vi-II in C major, but IV-ii-V in G major – the latter is a much more standard progression and ends with a recognised cadence. A modulation to G major has taken place.

In this extract from Beethoven's 4th String Quartet, the secondary dominant major supertonic 7th chord is boxed (the key is C minor):

In this case, the II7b is not followed **immediately** by chord V7 (G7). Instead, Beethoven inserts F#°7 (F#-A-C-Eb) and Ic, before the V7 chord arrives on the last beat of the bar. This is just a delaying process: F#°7 is very similar to D7, and Cm second inversion is very similar to V, (the bass note is the same, and Ic is often considered as a kind of appoggiatura on V).

ADDED 9TH CHORDS

Dominant chords may include an added 9th instead of (or as well as) the 7th. Dominant 9th chords also normally lead to the chord a perfect fifth lower, i.e. chord I.

A dominant 9th chord is likely to have one or more notes omitted. In C major, the full dominant 9th chord is G-B-D-F-A. Depending on how the chord is written, you could end up with G-A-B in close proximity to each other, which would sound like a muddy clash. For this reason, the third can be omitted. The 5th and 7th may also be omitted – there are several ways to write this chord (e.g. G-D-F-A, G-B-D-A etc.)

If you are asked to name a chord and at first glance it appears to be a random selection of notes, it could well be a V9 chord! To check, look at the bass note of the chord, and the following chord – a V9 chord will normally be followed by chord I in the exam (in real life, there are several other possibilities!) Stack the chord in 3rds, taking into account any missing notes. If you have a chord built on V with an added 9th, you have found your chord.

Here's an example of a V9 chord, from Chopin's "Minute Waltz". The key is Db major and the V9

chord contains the notes Ab-C-Gb-Bb. The 5th, Eb, is omitted. Notice that the notes Gb-Ab-Bb don't clash here, because there is quite a distance between them.

Dominant 7th chords are particularly helpful when modulating, because they always contain at least one note which is part of the **new** key but not part of the **old** one. E.g. when modulating from C major to a closely related key:

To the relative minor (A minor): V7 = E-B-G#-D (G# is not in the old key)

To the dominant key (G major): V7 = D-F#-A-C (F# is not in the old key)

To the subdominant key (F major): V7 = C-E-G-Bb (Bb is not in the old key)

And so on.

In tonal music, the **tonic** and **dominant** chords work together to "fix" a key. Within a melody, most of the notes falling on the **stronger** beats of the bar will be notes belonging to that key, and any chromatic (alien) notes are more likely to fall in between the beats.

So, in order to work out the **prevailing key** (i.e. the key of a piece of music at any point), look at the melody notes and work out which scale(s) they belong to, then look at the harmony and find chord V moving to chord I (or vice versa). When a piece of music is changing key, chord V7 is often used in place of the simpler chord V, so look out for that too. Chord vii° can also be used instead of V.

Usually when a piece changes key, accidentals will be introduced (or there could even be a change of key signature). An exception is when the music moves to the relative major e.g. Am moves to C major.

In this extract, which begins in the key of F minor, the music has modulated to Bb minor by bar 13:

V7d   ib   Vb   ia

The E natural in bar 11 is part of the key of F minor (it's the leading note from the harmonic minor scale). The circled B natural in bar 12 is an example of a **chromatic** auxiliary note – it is not part of the key (F minor).

At the end of bar 12, A natural is introduced, and the chord notes here are F-A-C-Eb (always stack the chord notes in **thirds** to find the correct chord name) so the chord is F major with an added 7th. In bar 13, the first chord is Bb minor (don't forget the Db in the key signature!) So at this point, the music has modulated to Bb minor, using V7-i.

If you are asked to locate a place in the music where a modulation takes place, begin by scanning for added accidentals. When you find accidentals, see which chords are formed, and whether they fit the particular modulation you are looking for.

The most common modulations are to the dominant, subdominant and relative major/minor key. You may see the term "**passing through**" – this is used for a very brief, transitory change of key which does not settle.

A fairly common chromatic chord, which you may well be asked to name or find, is the **Neapolitan 6th**.

This is a major chord, which is formed on the flattened supertonic, most often in minor key music.

For example, in the key of A minor, the **supertonic** note (second degree of the scale) is B. **Lower** this by a semitone to Bb, then make the **major** chord: Bb major. Most (but not all) of the time it's found in first inversion, which is why it's called a "6th" chord (as in figured bass, where first inversion chords are labelled "6"). The name "Neapolitan" comes from "Naples" in Italy, where it first became popular. Remember it as the major chord formed by moving up a semitone from the tonic chord.

It's usually notated as "N6" for convenience, although you could also describe it as bII.

Here is an example of a Neapolitan 6th from a Beethoven piano sonata. The key is D minor, so the N6 is a chord of Eb major. Here, it's in root position. Typically, the N6 chord is followed by a dominant chord.

The Diminished 7th Chord

Another common chromatic chord is the **diminished 7th**. This is a chord built solely of minor thirds, such as C-Eb-Gb-Bbb.

As with all chords, stack the chord's notes in **thirds** to find its **root**. For example here, from the bass upwards, we have the notes E-C#-G-Bb.

To find the root of the chord, we stack these in thirds to get C#-E-G-Bb, so this is a diminished 7th on C#.

Since the key is D minor, this chord is built on the 7th degree of the scale (vii). (We use lower case letters for chords which contain a minor third from the root). Add a small circle ° which means "diminished", and add the number "7" to show that there is an added 7th, so the chord is written as vii°7. Add the inversion (first inversion in this case), to get vii°7b.

In a minor key, chord ii° is also diminished, and so you may also come across diminished chords built on the second degree of the scale (ii°7).

In a **major** key piece, a diminished 7th chord built on vii° will also have an added accidental, for example in F major here, the diminished 7th chord is E-G-Bb-**Db**. This can be written as vii°b7, (with a "b7"), to show that the 7th has been lowered, or you can simply write "dim. 7th"! (Note: the ABRSM will actually accept "vii°7" for any type of diminished 7th chord.)

Augmented 6th Chords

There are three augmented 6th chords, named **Italian**, **French** and **German**. The French and German 6ths are four-note chords, and they can be considered as extended versions of the Italian 6th, which is a three note chord. The augmented 6th chords have a secondary dominant function, which means they normally lead to the dominant. These chords work equally well in major and minor keys.

To create an **Italian 6th** chord, start with the **tonic** note (let's say A in the key of A (major or minor). Add the note a major third lower (F), and then the note an augmented 6th higher than that (D#). Italian 6ths can be notated as "It6". Here is an Italian 6th in A minor. (Usually the tonic is doubled to create 4-part harmony.)

ia   It6   Va

To make a **French 6th**, add the supertonic note (B in A minor/major) to the Italian 6th. The notes in the French 6th sound dreamy, as they also happen to be part of the whole tone scale. Notate a French 6th as "Fr6".

To make a **German 6th**, take an Italian 6th, and add the note a minor third higher than the tonic, for example, C in the key of A minor/major. (So the note you add in a German 6th is actually one semitone higher than the note you add to make a French 6th). German 6th chords are often followed by a **second inversion** tonic chord, before the dominant – this is to avoid consecutive 5ths.

German 6ths sound the same as dominant 7ths out of context, but they are spelled a different way and don't sound like them in the context of a specific key. They are "enharmonic equivalent" chords – the same notes spelled in a different way.

The German 6th in A minor or A major is D#-F-A-C but the enharmonic dominant 7th is F-A-C-Eb. A German 6th will lead to V or Ic, whereas a dominant 7th will lead to I (Bb major in this case). Notate a German 6th as "Ger6".

GENERAL ADVICE ABOUT CHORDS

Although the vast majority of chords you are asked to find are dominant 7ths, diminished 7ths or Neapolitan 6ths, you can expect any "normal" chord to come up, including added 7th chords on any scale degree (not just the dominant). Chord iv7 is quite common, for example, or you may be asked to find an augmented triad, or a progression such as Ic-Va-Ia, in any stated key.

If you are asked to find a specific chord within a score, the wording is often something like *"find a dominant 7th chord in the relative major key"*.

- The first thing you need to do, is work out the **key** in question. For example, if the extract begins in Bb minor, first work out the "relative major key" part – it will be in Db major.
- Then work out what the dominant 7th in Db major is: Ab-C-Eb-Gb. These are the notes you are looking for.
- Now look at the **bass line** of the music – this is the easiest way to scan quickly for the information you need. Glue your eye to the part of the stave where Ab lives, and scan quickly looking for a note written in that place. As soon as you see an Ab, stop and check the rest of the chord. (Using this method works well, because you only have to concentrate on one part of the score, plus you are looking for something specific, rather than trying to analyse every chord you see!) Don't forget to check an octave higher or lower, if necessary, too. So in the bass clef, check for Ab on the bottom space, but also on the top line of the stave.
- If you fail to find the note you're looking for, repeat the process with the **next** chord note (C) in the triad, to see if the chord is in first inversion (you might be told which inversion to search for, in any case).

If you are asked to find an **augmented chord**, scan the extract for **accidentals.** There are no augmented triads which can occur **without** accidentals. An augmented chord contains a major third above the root, and an augmented 5th above the root, e.g. C-E-G#. Remember to stack the chord notes in thirds, to find out what the root is.

If you are asked to find a **Ic-Va progression**, it is easier if you know the key, but still pretty easy if you don't. In a Ic-Va progression, the **bass notes** in both chords always use the **same letter name**. Let's say you are asked to find the progression in the key of B major:

- Ic is a B major chord with **F# in the bass**, and
- Va is an F# major chord with **F# in the bass**.

You need to scan the **bass line** of the score, looking for two **consecutive** F#s. They may be in different octaves though, or they may be joined together as one long note, so look carefully.

If you don't know the key, you still need to scan the bass line looking for two **repeated notes or one held note**. If you fail to find two repeated notes or one held note, repeat the process but look for an **octave leap**. Then check that the chords fit.

You may be asked to say whether a given chord is an **enharmonic equivalent** of another chord. For example, is it true that this chord is an enharmonic equivalent of the dominant 7th in F major? The answer is yes! V7 in F major is C-E-G-Bb. This chord uses the same notes, with Bb spelled as A#.

6. RHYTHM

SYNCOPATION

In un-syncopated music, the **longer** notes fall on the **stronger** beats of the bar.

For example, in 12/8, one beat is worth one dotted crotchet (dotted quarter note), and there are four of them in each bar. So an un-syncopated rhythm could look like this:

In syncopated music, the longer notes are moved onto a weaker part of the bar, i.e. somewhere not falling **on the beat**. I've rewritten the above rhythm using the same lengths of notes, but pushed forward by a crotchet (quarter note). Now the longer notes fall on the **off beats**, and the rhythm is syncopated. (The **total value** of each note falling on the arrows here is the equivalent of a dotted crotchet (dotted quarter note)).

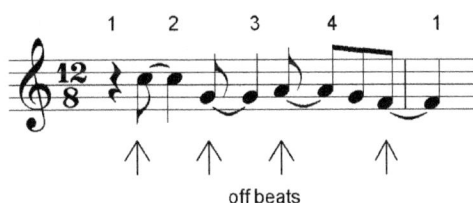

To find out whether a section of music is syncopated or not, first you need to look at the time signature and work out where the strong beats fall. Then decide whether the longer note values in the rhythm are **aligned** with the main beats. If they are not, then the music is syncopated.

In this example, both bars contain syncopation, in different ways:

In the first bar, the quaver (eighth note) A falls on a weaker beat than the shorter semiquavers (16th notes) either side of it. In the second bar, the tied Bs create a note worth ¾ of a beat, but this note falls just **before** beat 2, (which is the second strongest beat of the bar in 2/4).

ALTERNATIVE RHYTHMS

Some rhythms can be written in more than one way, with the same aural effect. For example, in compound time signatures, a duplet can be written as two dotted notes. These two rhythms are identical:

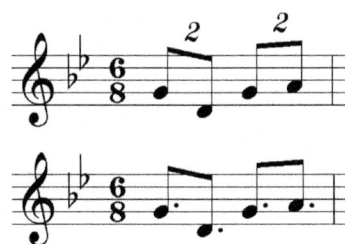

7. INSTRUMENT SPECIFICS

In this section we'll look at some of the instrument specific musical terminology and facts that have appeared in past papers for Grade 7.

This is not an exhaustive list however, and you should strive to increase your knowledge by studying musical scores as you listen along, and look up any unfamiliar words or symbols you find.

STRING INSTRUMENTS

Pizzicato (or pizz.) is an instruction to pluck the string with a finger, rather than the normal method of using the bow.

Arco is used after a pizzicato instruction, to show that the normal bowing method should be resumed.

V   Written above the stave, this is an "up bow" symbol, which means the player should push the bow upwards to play this note. Don't confuse it with an accent!

⊓   Also written above the stave, this is a "down bow" symbol – the player should draw the bow downwards to play the note.

°   This small circle symbol indicates that the player should lightly touch the string as he/she plays, in order to produce the effect of "harmonics". This allows higher partials of the note to be audible and changes the timbre of the sound produced.

Double and triple stop String instruments can play chords. When the player sounds two notes simultaneously, he/she draws the bow across two strings at the same time. A triple stop is a three-note chord. The following extract is from a violin part, showing triple stops.

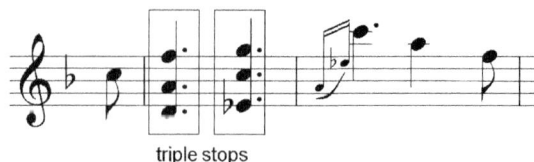

triple stops

Tremolando (or tremolo, or trem.) is a shimmering effect created by quickly alternating between up and down bows. The repeated notes are often marked with a slash, and the term **tremolando** (or one of its abbreviations) is always used in the exam papers. Don't confuse with "measured repeated notes"!

Sul means "on" and is used with the letter name of a particular string, to indicate that that string must be used. For example "sul G" means "use the G string".

Open string. String players get many different notes out of just one string, by placing their fingers on the string to make it shorter. This is called "stopping" the string. The lowest possible note that any string can produce is the note that sounds when it is not "stopped" at all – this is the "open string". Each string instrument has four strings, each with its own "open note".

You should learn the pitches of the strings of all four standard orchestral string instruments. Luckily, they are not difficult to remember! The viola and cello are tuned to the same notes, but the cello is an octave lower. The violin and double bass tunings are a mirror image of each other:

You may be asked whether, in an extract, a string player **"has to use"** an open string. Pay attention to the wording – it is not the same as **"could use"**. If a player **has to use** an open string it will be because:

- The extract contains the lowest playable note on that instrument (i.e. the open note on the lowest string) OR
- There is an instruction to use an open string (often marked with an "0" above the note) OR
- The indication "sul" (see above) matches up with a string's fundamental pitch. For example a notated D includes the instruction "sul D".

Look at these example viola notes, and consider whether the player **has to use an open string** or not:

1. No. The player *can* use an open string (the D string), but doesn't have to (they could play this as a stopped note on the lower pitched G string).

2. Yes. This is the lowest, and therefore unstopped, note on the indicated D string.

3. Yes. The "o" symbol indicates that an open string (the A string) must be used.

4. Yes. This is the lowest, and therefore unstopped, note on the instrument.

5. No. The player is instructed to play an E by stopping the D string.

HARP

Harp parts sometimes contain an instruction for the harpist to **set the pedals** to certain notes. Written between the staves, the tuning notes will be given. Make sure you know the note names in Italian, French and German as well as in English.

C=Do/Ut   D=Re   E=Mi   F=Fa   G=Sol   A=La   B=Si/H

Another standard harp term is "**glissando**" or "gliss." which is a rapid glide through several notes with a sweeping effect.

This extract shows a harp glissando, followed by a bar of silence in which the player retunes the pedals to E natural, B flat and A sharp. Notice the use of enharmonic equivalents (within the music (E#=F, B#=C) and the pedal instructions (Bb & A#)), which are quite common in harp music and facilitate playing the same note on different strings.

PIANO

In general, piano music is written on two staves combined with a curly brace at the left hand edge. The top stave is usually in the treble clef and intended for the right hand, whereas the lower stave is in the bass clef and intended for the left hand.

However, since the range of the piano is so wide, it's quite common to find the treble clef used for the left hand, when it's playing high notes, or for the bass clef to be used for the right hand, for low notes. Always check the clefs before you do anything else!

While most piano music is written for the right hand to play higher notes than the left, at times the pianist may be asked to **cross hands**, and at other times, the hands may be almost in exactly the same place. In these cases, the score will indicate which hand should be used.

Mano destra or "m.d." means "right hand" in Italian.

Mano sinistra or "m.s." means "left hand".

FRENCH HORN

French horn players place their right hand slightly inside the bell of the instrument during "normal" play. Sometimes the composer wants to make a more muffled sound, and will instruct the player to push their hand further inside the bell. This is notated with a plus or cross symbol +, and is called a "stopped note". An "o" symbol can be used, to clarify when an unstopped note is required.

TIMPANI

The two most common sounds produced from the timpani (or kettle drums) are the single stroke, and the characteristic timpani "roll". The roll is produced by rapidly striking the timp with alternate left and right mallets and is often used to create a feeling of drama or tension.

A roll can be indicated with the letters "**tr**" or notated as a slashed note.

In this example, the timpanist begins the roll very quietly and crescendos through until bar 3, which is accented:

Timpani drums need to be tuned to the correct pitch, so you may see a tuning indication within the score.

REED INSTRUMENTS

Often you will be asked to find something for example in a "single reed" or "double reed" part – so you need to know what type of reeds each instrument uses.

The oboe, bassoon and cor Anglais are all double reed instruments. This means they use two thin reeds which are bound together, and air is blown between the two reeds.

Clarinets (and saxophones – but they are not orchestral instruments) use a single reed. The player's breath is blown between the reed on one side, and the mouthpiece on the other.

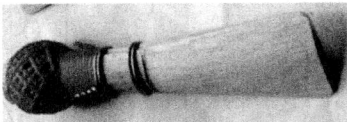

Bassoon double reed

Clarinet single reed and mouthpiece

8. COMPOSERS AND ERAS

In the Grade 7 music theory score reading question, you might be asked to name a likely **composer** or **era** for the score. The composers listed will be reasonably famous ones, and the musical eras are normally divided into 100-year options.

STYLISTIC CHARACTERISTICS & CLUES

1. Baroque (1600-1750)

- often polyphonic texture (using separate, rhythmically independent, intertwining melodies)
- "basso continuo" style with a keyboard accompanying solo instruments
- "suite" genre pieces (dances), including the minuet, gigue, sarabande, gavotte, bourée, allemande or courante
- period instruments such as harpsichord
- non-use of instruments not invented yet: piano, clarinet
- lack of dynamics and other performance directions
- simple harmony that mostly stays within one key or modulates to a closely related key
- use of ornaments such as turns, mordents etc.

2. Classical (1750-1820)

- light texture often with a solo melody against a chord-based accompaniment
- balanced form (e.g. regular 4-bar phrases)
- melodies based on scales/arpeggios
- harpsichord not typical
- piano and clarinet now in use
- small scale orchestras
- basic dynamics and simple performance directions such as accents, staccato
- tonal (diatonic) harmony with modulations to mostly closely related keys
- ornaments still in use, but less so
- pedal marks not used for piano

3. Romantic (1820-1900)

- rich, thick, dense texture (lots of notes at the same time)
- increasingly complex rhythms and cross-rhythms
- lyrical melodies
- many performance directions, highly expressive, dramatic and precise
- large scale orchestras often with additional non-standard instruments (e.g. contrabassoon)
- rapidly changing keys, often in unexpected directions, but still using the tonal (major/minor) system
- large contrasts in dynamics and articulations

4. Modern (1900-2000)

- dissonance
- non-standard notation e.g. dotted bar lines or absence of time signatures
- experimental techniques
- non-diatonic harmonies such as whole tone scales, atonalism, serialism, jazz harmony, experimental chords
- complex and irregular rhythms, frequently changing or unusual time signatures
- highly precise performance directions
- polytonality (using more than one key simultaneously)

Famous Composers

It's not possible to write an exhaustive list of composers whose names you should be familiar with, but here is a list of some of the names that have come up in Grade 7 music theory papers over the last few years:

Baroque (1600-1750) Purcell, Vivaldi, Bach, Handel,

Classical (1750-1820) Haydn, Mozart

Romantic (1820-1900) Beethoven, Rossini, Schubert, Mendelssohn, Chopin, Schumann, Verdi, Bruckner, Tchaikovsky, Dvorak, Wagner

Modern (1900-2000) Debussy, Ravel, Gershwin, Britten

You might be able to pinpoint a composer by the time period clues alone, but in other cases you may be presented with two or more composers from the **same** era. If so, you will need to know something more about the specific genres those composers were known for, or other clues.

Firstly, always look at the **language** used – while any composer might use Italian terms, only a German composer will use German terms, and only a French composer will use French. German composers include Wagner and Bruckner, French composers include Chopin, Ravel and Debussy.

Chopin wrote almost exclusively for the piano (including works for piano and orchestra).

Schubert is famous for writing **lieder** ("songs"). A **lied** is usually for a solo voice with a simple, elegant piano accompaniment, and is written in German.

Verdi and **Rossini** are known for writing opera and oratorios.

Gershwin wrote jazzy harmonies.

Debussy had a preference for the whole tone scale (e.g. C-D-E-F#-G#-A#)

Bruckner, Mahler and **Wagner** were famous for using enormous, extended orchestras.

9. TRANSPOSITION

One question which is highly likely to come up in the grade 7 music theory exam is **French horn transposition** – make sure you know exactly how to do it! You might also get a transposition question for clarinet, cor Anglais or trumpet, or you may be asked to transpose into a different **clef**, as in earlier grades.

Cors Anglais and most **French horns** are pitched in F. To transpose into concert pitch, transpose **down a perfect 5th**. You may need to transpose from treble to bass clef as well as transposing the pitch – make sure you keep the correct octave of the notes, relative to middle C. French horns can occasionally appear in keys other than F – so be vigilant!

Clarinets are pitched in Bb or A. Remember that the Italian terms are sib and la, and the German word for Bb is "*B*"! (There is no such thing as a clarinet in B). Clarinets should also be transposed **down** – a **major 2nd** for Bb clarinets, or a **minor 3rd** for clarinets in A. (The small-sized clarinet in Eb transposes **up a minor 3rd** into concert pitch – I've never seen this instrument required for transposition at grade 7 though).

Trumpets are usually (but not always) pitched in Bb, and work the same way as clarinets in Bb.

At this grade, the transposition questions are normally a bit more complicated than in earlier grades, and you will need to make sure your notation is 100% correct, as well as the pitches. This includes:

- aligning multiple parts correctly on the vertical axis
- putting stems, slurs and ties the correct way round according to the normal principles
- noticing whether there is a key signature to take into account, or not

Can you see one mistake the in following French horn transposition? The answer is at the bottom of the page! [3]

Original   Transposition

---

[3] Answer: the second crotchet (quarter note) G in the bass clef should **not** be aligned with the quavers (eighth notes) in treble clef.

ENHARMONIC TRANSPOSITION

Very occasionally, the key you transpose into might be an **enharmonic** equivalent. For example, if a Bb clarinet part is originally in the key of Gb major, if you transpose it down a major 2nd, you will arrive at the key of Fb major. Obviously it makes no sense to write something in Fb major, when you could write it in E major instead. In cases like this, the actual interval of transposition will be different – Gb-E is a diminished 3rd. Look at the key signature on the answer stave before you begin!

In this example, the Bb clarinet part is in Gb major and the answer stave has a key signature for E major.

The correct answer is this:

And not this – imagine playing all those flats within a sharp key signature!

SCORE READING EXERCISES

Look at the orchestral extract on the next page and answer the following questions.

1. Find a pedal which lasts for two bars, and mark it with a bracket and the letter A.

2. Write out the horn part in bars 42-44 as it would sound at concert pitch.

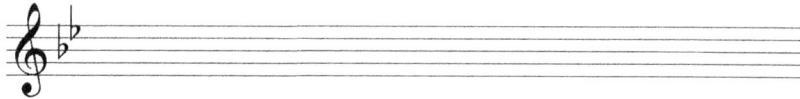

3. Write out the clarinet parts in bars 43-45 as they would sound at concert pitch.

4. Describe how the timpani player would play bar 44.

5. Find a melodic interval of a compound perfect 5th (perfect 12th), and mark it with a bracket and the letter B.

6. Find a harmonic interval of minor 7th played by the same instruments, and mark it with the letter C.

7. Describe how the second half of bar 50 in the viola part will sound.

8. What key has the music reached by the end of this extract?

9. Explain "a2" (e.g. in the oboe part bar 43).

10. Find an example of syncopation in unison between two different instruments, from bar 45 onwards. Mark it with a box and the letter D.

11. Which two standard orchestral brass instruments are not used in this extract?

12. Rewrite the bassoon part in bars 38-39, using the tenor clef. Do not change the pitch.

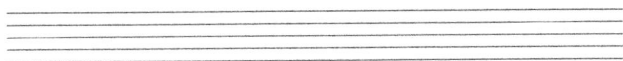

13. True or false: the violin I part has to use the lowest available note on the instrument.

14. How is a contrast achieved in bar 42 onwards, compared to the previous 4 bars?

15. What does "sf" mean (bar 39)?

16. Which of the following periods is the most likely time of composition? 1600-1700, 1700-1800, 1800-1900 or 1900-2000? Give reasons for your answer.

17. Which of the following is the most likely composer of this piece: Debussy, Chopin, Haydn or Mahler?

18. Give the note value name (e.g. crotchet/quarter note) of the fastest note used in this extract.

19. In total, how many woodwind players are required in this extract?

20. True or false: the cellos and double basses play at exactly the same pitch throughout this extract.

Flauti
Oboi
Clarinetti in la
Fagotti
Corni in fa
Trombe in re
Timpani in re/la
Violino I
Violino II
Viola
Violoncello e c. basso
a2
Fl.
Ob.
Fg.
sempre ff

SCORE READING ANSWERS

1. Bassoon part, bars 40-41.
2.

3.

4. The player would perform a roll on the note A – rapidly alternating the mallets.
5. Violin I part, bar 42.
6. Oboe part, bar 50.
7. Repeated, measured semiquavers (16th notes) played as a double stop.
8. Bb major.
9. Both players to play the same part.
10. Flute/oboes bars 48-49
11. Trombone and tuba.
12.

13. False.
14. Key change from Gm to Dm, fuller orchestra employed (brass, strings and percussion added), dynamic contrast ff from pp, rhythm faster with semiquavers (16th notes) used.
15. "Sforzando" means forced, accented
16. 1700-1800. It is typical of the "classical" era style because of:
    *   Small sized orchestra
    *   Mainly homophonic rather than polyphonic
    *   Basic performance directions included, without being too specific
    *   Elegant, light style, rather than emotional/heavy
    *   Tonal harmony, with modulations only to closely related keys
17. Haydn (the extract is from Haydn's Symphony no. 104, second movement)
18. Demisemiquaver (32nd note)
19. 8 (2 flutes, 2 oboes, 2 clarinets and 2 bassoons)
20. False: (because the double bass sounds an octave lower than written).

ACKNOWLEDGEMENTS

"Bassoon Reeds". Licensed under CC BY-SA 3.0 via Wikimedia Commons - https://commons.wikimedia.org/wiki/File:Bassoon_Reeds.jpg#/media/File:Bassoon_Reeds.jpg

"Clarinet Reed and Mouthpiece" By James Eaton-Lee Njan [GFDL (http://www.gnu.org/copyleft/fdl.html) or CC-BY-SA-3.0 (http://creativecommons.org/licenses/by-sa/3.0/)], via Wikimedia Commons

Printed in Great Britain
by Amazon